Portrait Life of Lincoln

Portrait Life of Lincoln

Life of Abraham Lincoln, the Greatest American, told from Original Photographs taken with His Authority during the Great Crisis through which He Led His Country—Treasured among the 7000 Secret Service War Negatives in the Brady-Gardner Collection at Springfield, Massachusetts, and in Private Collections, valued at $150,000 Collected by Edward Bailey Eaton

By

FRANCIS TREVELYAN MILLER

Founder and Editor-in-Chief of " The Journal of American History "
Author of " The Photographic History of the Civil War "
Author of " American Hero Tales "—Editor of the Search-Light Library
Member of The American Historical Association
Fellow of The American Geographical Society
Member of The American Statistical Association
Member of The National Geographic Society
Member of The American Academy of Political and Social Science

Anno Domini   SPRINGFIELD, MASSACHUSETTS   Mcmx

The Patriot Publishing Company

NEW YORK, 439 Lafayette Street   Marquette Building, CHICAGO

F O R E W O R D

IT is with pleasure that this volume is presented to the American people as a direct and original contribution to our national literature. As a collection of the famous portraits of Lincoln, taken from the greatest collections in the world and valued at more than $150,000, it alone would claim distinction. This is the first collection of all the known original photographs of Lincoln and represents years of research by the most eminent American collectors.

It is, however, upon its graphic literary treatment that this volume must take its position as one of the most important books of the times. It is a book with a mission—and that mission is to revive in the homes of America the true spirit of Lincoln; that man of rugged honesty who said that "God must have loved the common people or he would not have made so many of them;" the man who "knew what it meant to start at the bottom and work to the top;" the man who "met misfortune face to face and overcame it with the might of manhood." Its psychological insight into human nature; its philosophical grasp on life and its opportunities; its appeal to the American heart and conscience, with its vigorous application of the principles of Lincoln to everyday life, inspire one with new courage and new ambition.

Lincoln lives again in the pages of this volume, through the portraits and the word paintings that are masterpieces of literary art. It has been the desire of the publishers to make it a new American classic in which the generations may look upon Lincoln in the most dramatic situations in his life, feeling the impulse of a great heart and the inspiration of an indomitable will and resolute purpose.

More books have been written about Lincoln than any other man in the world's history, but this is the first time that he has been brought before the people in the actual negatives for which he sat during his life and in text pictures in which he again moves among us. It has been the purpose of the publishers to present, in the fewest possible pages, a full acquaintance with Lincoln and an understanding of what such a man means to the world of humanity. It has further been desired to make this a complete unfolding of the vital events in his life. This has been accomplished by an interesting chronology in which the whole panorama of the growth of the nation, during the life of Lincoln, is presented. The volume further includes the nine great speeches upon which Lincoln rose to the highest political honor within the gift of the American people. These, with a record of the celebrated Lincoln Collections in America, and the hundred greatest books on Lincoln, fulfill its title as the "Portrait Life of Lincoln," and give it immediate position as the first authoritative handbook on Lincoln.

THE PUBLISHERS

C O N T E N T S

PART I

An Epigrammatic Philosophy on Life and Its Opportunities Drawn from
the Early Experiences of Abraham Lincoln

THE ROAD TO GREATNESS.. 3
THE FULLNESS OF LIFE AND OPPORTUNITY—BIRTH.......................... 4
THE JOYS AND SORROWS OF LIVING—CHILDHOOD............................ 5
THE UNFOLDING OF KNOWLEDGE—SCHOOL DAYS.............................. 6
THE REVELATION OF LIFE'S SECRETS—BOYHOOD 7
THE THRILL OF AMBITION—YOUTH... 8
THE DISCOVERY OF POWER—CITIZENSHIP.................................. 9
THE COURAGE OF CONVICTION—MANHOOD................................... 10

PART II

A Photographic Narrative Which Interprets the Character and Life of
Abraham Lincoln, the Greatest American

THE FOUNDATION OF LINCOLN'S CHARACTER................................ 12
THE INFLUENCE OF LOVE ON LINCOLN'S LIFE.............................. 14
THE POLITICAL PRINCIPLES OF LINCOLN................................. 16
THE IMPULSE THAT HELD LINCOLN STEADFAST............................. 18
THE RUGGED HONESTY OF LINCOLN'S HEART............................... 20
THE MAN WHO FIRST MADE LINCOLN KNOWN 22
THE CHALLENGE THAT TESTED LINCOLN'S STRENGTH........................ 24
THE DEFEAT THAT MADE LINCOLN FAMOUS................................. 26
THE APPEAL OF HUMANITY THAT LINCOLN HEARD........................... 28
THE FIRST TEST OF LINCOLN'S NATIONAL GREATNESS...................... 30
THE INSPIRATION OF LINCOLN'S PATRIOTISM............................. 32
THE GATHERING OF HUMANITY UNDER LINCOLN............................. 34
THE BURDEN OF A NATION ON LINCOLN'S HEART........................... 36
THE AFFECTION OF LINCOLN FOR HIS HOME............................... 38
THE WILLINGNESS OF LINCOLN TO GIVE HIS LIFE......................... 42
THE FORTITUDE OF LINCOLN IN HOUR OF TRIAL........................... 44
THE CRUMBLING NATION IN LINCOLN'S ARMS.............................. 46
THE DETERMINED WILL OF LINCOLN AMONG MEN............................ 48
THE TRUE TEST OF LINCOLN'S STATESMANSHIP............................ 50
THE STRENGTH OF LINCOLN IN A NATION'S PERIL......................... 52
THE FAITH OF LINCOLN IN THE COMMON PEOPLE........................... 54
THE ABILITY OF LINCOLN TO OVERCOME DEFEAT........................... 56
THE HOPEFULNESS OF LINCOLN IN MISFORTUNE............................ 58
THE MIGHT OF LINCOLN IN HIS COUNTRY'S CRISIS........................ 64
THE HAND OF LINCOLN ON THE CHAIN OF BONDAGE......................... 66
THE GREATEST SACRIFICE OF LINCOLN'S LIFE............................ 68
THE POWER OF LINCOLN TO CONQUER HIMSELF............................. 70
THE HUMILITY OF LINCOLN IN HOUR OF VICTORY.......................... 72
THE SYMPATHY OF LINCOLN FOR THE UNFORTUNATE......................... 76
THE WORTH OF A MAN IN LINCOLN'S JUDGMENT............................ 78

CONTENTS

THE LOYALTY OF LINCOLN TO HIS LIFE WORK.................................... 80

THE INSIGHT OF LINCOLN INTO HUMAN NATURE................................. 84

THE HEART OF LINCOLN THAT KNEW NO MALICE................................. 86

THE FATHERHOOD OF LINCOLN AMONG THE LOWLY.............................. 88

THE MAGNANIMITY OF THE SPIRIT OF LINCOLN.................................. 90

THE VICTORY OF LINCOLN—A RE-UNITED PEOPLE............................... 92

THE VEIL OF SORROW OVER AN EXULTANT NATION............................. 94

PART III

A Revelation of the Last Scenes in the Closing Hours of Lincoln from
Actual Photographs Taken at the Time

THE LAST LINGERING MOMENTS OF A NOBLE LIFE............................... 96

THE MAGNIFICENCE OF LIFE'S LAST TRIUMPH.................................. 98

THE INFAMY OF A DEED THAT ROBBED A NATION.............................. 100

THE GLORY OF A MAN WHO LOVES HIS FELLOWMEN........................... 106

PART IV

The Great Speeches that Mark the Rise of Abraham Lincoln as
an Orator and Leader of the People

THE FIRST PUBLIC SPEECH OF ABRAHAM LINCOLN............................... 112

THE FIRST GREAT PATRIOTIC SPEECH OF LINCOLN.............................. 113

THE FIRST GREAT NATIONAL SPEECH OF LINCOLN.............................. 119

THE SPEECHES IN LINCOLN'S POLITICAL GREATNESS........................... 132

THE SPEECH THAT MOLDED A NATION'S FUTURE................................ 133

THE GREATEST SPEECH IN AMERICAN HISTORY................................. 139

THE LAST PUBLIC SPEECH OF ABRAHAM LINCOLN.............................. 141

THE WORDS OF WISDOM FROM LINCOLN'S PHILOSOPHY......................... 144

PART V

A Chronology of the Historic Events in the Growth of the American
Nation from the Birth to the Death of Lincoln

THE CHRONOLOGY OF THE LIFE OF LINCOLN.................................... 145

PART VI

A Handbook of the Famous Photographic Portraits of Abraham Lincoln
Treasured in the Great American Collections

THE FAMOUS PORTRAITS OF LINCOLN WITH COMPLETE INDEX TO ALL PHOTOGRAPHS
REPRODUCED IN THIS VOLUME... 155

THE BIBLIOGRAPHY OF ABRAHAM LINCOLN—THE HUNDRED GREATEST BOOKS ON HIS
LIFE 161

THE GREATEST POEM ON LINCOLN—O CAPTAIN! MY CAPTAIN!—BY WALT WHITMAN . 164

INTRODUCTORY

AS an American, who loves his country and his people, I believed that I knew Lincoln. Throughout my life I have read the anecdotes and biographies that make him familiar to the generations, but it was not until I looked upon his portraits that I began to understand the real character of the man. It was then, as Bartlett, the sculptor, has said, that I looked into a face in which is written the history of a nation and the hopes of its people—the face of democracy.

There is always something about an old photograph that is intensely human. In it still lives one who has been long absent; the expression on the face, the light in the eyes, the kindness and the firmness of the mouth. One can almost feel the heart that beat beneath it. So it was that, in these photographs, I found the living Lincoln. My acquaintance with him before had been only through the various estimates of his character. I believe that there are more than two thousand of them, including many masterly biographies, in which one listens to the men who knew him and hears reminiscences of his drollery and wit.

But it is in these time-stained photographs that the man comes back to us. About them gather all the events of his life. Look at that familiar picture of the old log cabin where he was born. In your imagination you can see the great forests, and the sunshine in the trees; you can see the little creeping figure before the door; it is a baby; it laughs and cries. Look, look again; now it is a boy; he runs and jumps and shouts; he is standing at the opening of the woods; he is shielding his eyes with his hands and looking this way; he is calling to us; he is waving his arms; he is coming down the forest path, under the great trees, nearer and nearer. Look again—he stands right before us; he is a man!

And now, taking up his first photograph, look into the youthful face filled with hope and courage. In it you can see the storms that are gathering about his life. One by one these old portraits unfold the life story of the man who gave his personality to them—they are all that remain of the physical Lincoln.

Sit down with me and turn these pages in reverie. In your mind's eye you can see the gaunt figure in the law office; you sit with him as he pores over his books during that long, weary period of a lawyer's life—waiting for clients; you fight with him as a captain in the Black Hawk War; you take your letters to him as the village postmaster; you cast your ballot for him as a member of the state legislature; you see him take his first stand against slavery. Now you are listening to his convincing oratory against the great Douglas for the senate; those ringing words are dropping from his lips: "You can fool all of the people some of the time, and some of the people all of the time, but you cannot fool all of the people all of the time."

In this reverie over these old portraits you can hear the cheering; he

INTRODUCTORY

is being nominated for the presidency. You are standing beside him as he receives the news that he has been elected to the highest political honor in the gift of mankind—the leadership of the American people; you listen to his farewell speech to his friends at Springfield; you go with him to Washington and sit with him in the White House; you hear the news of the first shot at Fort Sumter; you hear the clank of the cavalry and the tramp of regiments of marching men offering their lives on the altar of civilization; you sit silent with him in the gloom of defeat; you catch the gleam of light in the din of victory; you gaze bewildered upon him as he issues the Emancipation Proclamation. Now you are going with him to Antietam, to Gettysburg, to Richmond; you are standing beside him as he hears the news of the surrender at Appomattox. The soldiers are passing through the streets of Washington on their homeward march, and your foot beats time to the strains of the "Star Spangled Banner" and "Dixie."

The pages are now nearly turned. The last portrait is before you. A shot rings in your ears; a figure falls prostrate to the floor; you linger by his bedside through the long hours; Seward is whispering: "Now he belongs to the ages." You stand over the bier and look upon the kindly face that you have learned to love; you heap his grave with flowers. This is the "Portrait Life of Lincoln."

In simple words I have endeavored to gather about these old portraits the scenes in which the living Lincoln stood at the time that the photographs were taken. I have neither the desire nor the ability to make this volume a biography of Lincoln nor a history of the times in which he lived. It is but a series of word-pictures and life-portraits in which you may look upon Lincoln and come to your own conclusion regarding his strength of character and his greatness as a man.

It has seemed to me, after looking upon them, that in this man we find the strongest character that American civilization has produced. I know no other man in American history who has been called upon to meet such overwhelming obstacles and who has overcome them with truer courage, finer fortitude, and greater self-sacrifice. This is the man who led his people through the greatest crisis that the American Nation has known. I believe that when one considers that the United States exist today largely through the faith and hope and indomitable will of this man, he may justly be entitled "The Greatest American."

It is not my privilege, however, to fix the historical position of Lincoln. I shall be satisfied if my humble service is but to bring the generations into personal acquaintance with him, for it is in his character that they will find the whole secret of the power of common manhood. The strength with which he faced the problems of life is an inspiration to all men; it is the hope of the future; the convincing proof of the ability of the common man

INTRODUCTORY

to rise above his surroundings and make his way in the world through the courage of his convictions. It is the very simplicity of Lincoln as a man that brings him so close to us. He is the most companionable of men. In him you find many of your own characteristics—the common qualities of human nature. To know Lincoln is to know yourself. He is the common heritage of the American people.

In these introductory words I desire to express my appreciation to those who have assisted in giving me a clear understanding of the man whose portraits are here presented in photograph and text. I am especially indebted to Honorable Robert Todd Lincoln, of Chicago, Illinois, who has advised me regarding the sources for original investigation, and to Mr. Edward Bailey Eaton, of Hartford, Connecticut, who, in his untiring historical research, has collected these photographs and has collaborated with me in preparing "The Portrait Life of Lincoln."

I further desire to give credit to the collectors who have rendered assistance. The Frederick H. Meserve Collection of Americana, in New York, and the Fay Collection of photographs of historic personages, in Illinois, are among the most valuable collections in America. The Oldroyd Lincoln Memorial Collection, which now occupies the historic house in which Lincoln died, at Washington, is a shrine that should be visited by every American. Among its treasures are nearly twenty thousand exhibits relating to the life of the great American. The Lambert Collection, in Philadelphia, is the work of one of the leading authorities on Lincolniana. Many original negatives are treasured in the Handy and the Rice Collections in Washington.

The largest collection of original Civil War negatives is the famous Brady-Gardner Collection, in Springfield, Massachusetts, which contains more than seven thousand negatives taken under the protection of the Secret Service during the American Crisis. The only other collection of its magnitude is deposited in the War Department at Washington, where it is held as official documentary evidence of this great epoch in American history. In these collections can be found practically everything pertaining to the life and character of Abraham Lincoln.

The author takes pleasure in commending these collections to the American people and acknowledging the valuable services extended by all who have co-operated in preparing this volume, which we trust may bring the generations closer to the heart and ideals of the world's greatest apostle of common manhood—Abraham Lincoln.

Francis Trevelyan Miller

"Buena Vista"
Hartford, Connecticut

Dedicated to the United States of America, the only land on earth where a man can rise from a cabin to the palace within the hearts of a Great People

The Portrait Life of Lincoln

PART I

An Epigrammatic Philosophy on Life and
Its Opportunities drawn from
the Early Experiences of
Abraham Lincoln

The Life-Mask of Abraham Lincoln

This bronze doth keep the very form and mold
      Of our great martyr's face. Yes, this is he;
      That brow all wisdom, all benignity;
That human, humorous mouth; those cheeks that hold
Like some harsh landscape all the summer's gold;
      That spirit fit for sorrow, as the sea
      For storms to beat on; the lone agony
Those silent, patient lips too well foretold.
Yes, this is he who ruled a world of men
      As might some prophet of the elder day—
      Brooding above the tempest and the fray
With deep-eyed thought and more than mortal ken.
      A power was his beyond the touch of art
      Or armed strength—his pure and mighty heart.
            —*From poems of Richard Watson Gilder.*

THE ROAD TO GREATNESS

Philosophy of the Life of Lincoln

THE *Greatest Man in the World* is not the man who accumulates the most money or the most power; it is not the man who takes the most out of life; it is the man who gives the most to life. The world is a great harvest-house of man's bounteous industry. Death garners the crops which he has sown. His true riches are estimated, not by that which he leaves to his sons, but by that which he leaves to his fellow-men as a heritage for the generations to come.

Life is a journey between the starting point of Decision and the far-away mountain heights of Ambition. The path is long and tortuous. It leads down through the dark and dismal swamps of Indecision, and over the rough and stony hills of Disappointment. There loom in the pathway the jagged cliffs of Discouragement that seem almost impossible to climb. Below them is the deep abyss of Lost Hope. There are crossroads of Temptation; and rivers of Sorrow to ford.

It takes a strong man to make the journey; one who knows the forests, who has been hardened to the storms; who knows Nature because he has lived close to its heart. It is the rugged country boy, with his face tanned by the winds, his muscles strengthened by hard labor, and his heart full of sunshine and cheerfulness as its own beacon light, that makes the most courageous journeyman. It needs one whose will has been beaten into steel on the forge of life; one who knows the sweet peace of the rest that follows fatigue and suffering; one who has no fear because he has many times met danger face to face—and overcome it. He knows that just beyond the gloomy clouds the golden light of life still shines; he knows the truth of the old adage, that it is darkest just before the dawn.

The abyss of Time holds the millions that have been too weak for the journey; those who wandered in the glamour of luxury and ease—only to be lost. Far beyond, on the pinnacles that pierce the sky, where the glorious sun casts a halo about them, are the strong who have gained the heights and live forever in the sublime light of Immortality. Among them are many who were without worldly possessions and were counted poor on earth. Few, indeed, are there who were rich and powerful. Not one is among them who purchased his way with tributes of gold and silver.

Courage, Fortitude, Sacrifice, Sympathy, Love—these are the price of Immortal Greatness; they lie in the heart of man.

THE FULLNESS OF LIFE AND OPPORTUNITY—BIRTH

*I*T *is with this measure of a man* that we look upon the American boy who journeyed from the humblest log home, along the road of life, to an everlasting abiding-place in the heart of humanity; who overcame the greatest obstacles that can beset man; who carried on his shoulders a burden that weighed down the world.

There is not one who reads these lines who was born in humbler circumstances than Abraham Lincoln; not one whose opportunities in life are so limited as those which surrounded him; and yet he became one of the greatest of men. His life proves to all generations the power of an indomitable will and a resolute purpose; that man, when he conquers himself, can conquer the world.

Do you remember that old homestead where you were born? It was a mansion compared with that rough log cabin in the Kentucky wilderness where Abraham Lincoln began life on that cold winter day on the twelfth of February, in 1809.

Do you remember the dear old village where you spent your childhood days; its long country roads, shaded with towering maples and elms, along which you romped and shouted and played on your way to school—those good old days in the country? It was a great world of light and laughter, of pleasure and friendship, of wonderful opportunities, compared with that forest home of Abraham Lincoln where only the growl of the bear echoed along the trail, where the ring of the ax was the only sound of civilization, and desolation and poverty were his only friends—and they were staunch friends.

Every American is rich today in comparison with the worldly possessions of Abraham Lincoln during his childhood, his youth, and his early manhood—rich in surroundings of home; rich in the comforts of life; rich in the opportunities for learning and education. There is not an American youth who is not a millionaire in the possibilities of vast success in life, compared to the possibilities that were within the grasp of Abraham Lincoln on the day that he left his father's roof to go out into the great world, of which he knew only the knowledge that comes from the school of the woods and the motherhood of Nature. There was one thing that he did not know and never learned—and that was Fear. He learned early that man is his own master; that with a strong arm, a strong heart, and a strong will, there is no power on earth that he need fear; that with his conscience clear and his mind clean the future will take care of itself and even Death is conquered.

THE JOYS AND SORROWS OF LIVING—CHILDHOOD

THE *safest capital on which to begin life* is good health and sound morals. With these, permanent failure is almost impossible. There is not money enough in the banks of the world to buy them. In partnership with Industry and Thrift, they must succeed. Any man who possesses them has the wealth of the world within his reach. Education, social position, political power, financial credit—all these, then, but await your desire.

This is the capital upon which Abraham Lincoln began. His father was a woodsman who could neither read nor write; his mother was an orphan girl. His cabin home of rough-hewn logs sheltered but a single room; but here, on the banks of Nolen Creek, in desolate Hardin County, he started on life's journey.

Do you remember the first time that you left home? How you bade good-by to the old scenes? How you turned and looked back for one last lingering glance at the old place that you loved—and then wiped a tear away? You know, then, what it meant to the seven-year-old Lincoln when, with his little sister, he trudged behind his father and mother from the Kentucky wilds into southern Indiana, where, with an ax, they cut their way through the dense forests to start life anew.

Here, in the savage wilds of Little Pigeon Creek, they felled the trees for a new cabin. The bare earth, which turned to mud in the winter thaws, was its floor. There were no windows to let in the sunlight and not even a skin to hang over the doorway to shut out the sleet and snow. The little lad fell asleep on the heap of loose leaves—and he called it *home*.

Do you remember the first great sorrow that came into your life? The loved one whose lips you kissed for the last time? Whose eyes were never to look again into yours? Whose hand as you clasped it in your own was cold and white? You know, then, the grief that lay in the heart of this lad as he knelt sobbing beside his dying mother. You can feel, then, the touch of her hand as she laid it on his young head and whispered the last message from those loving lips: "Be good to your father and sister. Be kind to one another—and worship God." Your heart goes out to him as they lay her away in a rough box, hewn from the pine forest, and tenderly lower her to the resting place on the knoll where the sunlight pours its golden wreaths upon her grave. You know what was in his heart when in after years he bowed his head and called her *"My angel mother."*

THE UNFOLDING OF KNOWLEDGE—SCHOOL DAYS

LIFE'S lessons are not all learned in a university. Poverty, toil, suffering—these are the schools of discipline, and the man who passes through them has an education that all the universities of the earth could not give. The book of Nature does not teach the conjugation of verbs; it teaches the conjugation of life. It may not master the tongues of dead languages, but it does master the tongues of the thousand living languages—the language of the Heart, of the Hand, of Common Sense. It may not lead to a doctorate in science, but it does lead to the highest degree within the power of man—the degree of *strong character.*

The backwoods is the university that made Lincoln. Here he learned a lesson that few men ever learn—how to bear the burdens of life without complaint, and how to overcome them.

At ten years of age, he was walking nine miles a day to and from the little log schoolhouse in the woods. At night, he lay before the fireplace ciphering on a wooden shovel and scrawling his name on the logs of the cabin. A new world had been revealed to him—the world of knowledge. Within his humble home there had never been a newspaper or a story book, but now he had made the first great discovery of his life. He had found that within the covers of books lay the secrets that unlock the mysteries of the earth; that through them you can sit in the comradeship and listen to the wisdom of the wise men of the ages; that with them you cannot be alone, for the intimate friendship of the world's greatest men is yours.

This is the education that is within the reach of every man, woman and child in America today—the university of outdoor life and of books.

Do you remember the first book that you ever read? Possibly it was Æsop's Fables or Bunyan's "Pilgrim's Progress," or "Robinson Crusoe." These were the books that kindled the flame of desire in Lincoln's mind, until, at nineteen years of age, although his total schooling was less than a year, he had read every book that he could borrow within fifty miles of his home.

This was Lincoln's education. There he stood, long, lank, swarthy; six feet four inches tall; strong as a giant, a heart like the oak, and a head full of Common Sense—ready and eager to fight it out with Destiny.

THE REVELATION OF LIFE'S SECRETS—BOYHOOD

CHOOSING *an occupation is the first great crisis in life.* Many a good farmer is spoiled in the making of a lawyer, and so it is through all the trades and life professions. There is in each one of us some natural tendency toward certain lines of work, and success depends largely upon giving heed to this warning. Whatever line of work you may choose there is always some opportunity to reach the top.

Abraham Lincoln did not choose his calling; he allowed it to choose him. He passed the apprenticeship of hard work and answered the call of duty wherever he found it. He was a wood chopper and a farm hand; he swung the ax and the scythe, slaughtered hogs and wielded the flail. A day's work was from sunrise to sunset. The pay, which was a quarter of a dollar, went to his father, to whom he owed all his time until noon of his twenty-first birthday. A ferryman offered thirty-seven cents a day for his services, on the deck as a bow hand, to help pole the craft down the Ohio and Mississippi to New Orleans. This was his first real revelation of the great channels of trade and commerce. He realized for the first time that he lived in a great world of throbbing humanity in which every man is trying to make the most of his short journey through it. He began to feel the beat of the human heart and the pulse of life itself. The great brotherhood of man, with its laughter and tears, gripped at his heart; and he found himself a man among men.

Do you remember the thrill that you felt when you earned the first dollar that was to be your very own? No matter what success may come to you, or whatever fortune you may accumulate, you will never be as rich as that again. It was this same feeling that Lincoln felt when in after life he told the story.

"I was about eighteen years of age," he said. "Two men hailed me and asked me to take their trunks to a steamer which waited for them in midstream. I sculled them out to the steamer. They got on board, and I lifted the trunks and put them on the deck. The steamer was about to put on steam again, when I called out, 'You have forgotten to pay me.' Each of them took from his pocket a silver half dollar and threw it on the bottom of my boat. You may think it was a very little thing, and in these times it seems to me like a trifle, but it was a most important incident in my life. I could scarcely credit that I, the poor boy, had earned a dollar in less than a day; that by honest work I had earned a dollar. I was a more hopeful and thoughtful boy from that time."

THE THRILL OF AMBITION—YOUTH

EVERY *man must make his own place in the world.* There is no one who will do it for him. It takes good grit to hew your way to the front. Abraham Lincoln started out into the world with an ax over his shoulder. An ox team had drawn the family and its scanty possessions from Indiana to Illinois. The wagon wheels were but round blocks of wood cut from the trunk of an oak tree, with a hole in the center for the axle. He was now twenty-two years of age, and, having helped build the new home in the wilderness, he bid good-by to his father and stood alone in the world—his own master and his own servant.

Look—far down the road you can see that tall, gaunt, sad-faced youth; his coat ragged; his hat battered; his trousers of torn and patched homespun—and, as he passes from view, you feel that one not wholly unlike yourself has passed by; that if he, with only struggle behind him and struggle ahead of him, has the courage to fight it out with the might of manhood, then you cannot stand by as an idler and a coward.

The experiences that Lincoln met were those that we all meet in the necessity of earning a livelihood. He took whatever honest occupation came to him; he split rails; he became a flatboatman; he worked in the country store at New Salem, a village of twenty log houses,—and more than all, he left kindness wherever he went. He watched with the sick; if a widow were in need of firewood he would cut it for her; if he made a mistake in weight or change, he did not sleep until he had corrected the error—and through this he received the first and highest honor of his life, the title of "Honest Abe."

There comes a day to each of us when we decide whether we are to be the leader or the follower of men. With Lincoln, as with many youths today, it was his physical prowess. Remarkable stories were told of his giant strength, of his picking up and moving a chicken house weighing 600 pounds, and how he could raise a barrel from the ground and lift it until, standing erect, he could drink from the bunghole, and by means of ropes and straps fastened about his hips he could lift a box of stones weighing nearly 1000 pounds; but his first real victory came when he thrashed the chief bully of the village and won the admiration and respect of the community. It was this that resulted in his being chosen captain in the Black Hawk War, and sent his fame broadcast through the frontier settlements. It is as true today as it was then, that, whether it be in brawn or brain, it is the survival of the fittest.

THE DISCOVERY OF POWER—CITIZENSHIP

*T*HE *man who is not interested in public affairs* cannot hope to succeed. He has no right to either complain or ask help, for he has deliberately shut himself off from the world. In this great brotherhood of men, which we call a democracy, every man is pledged upon his honor to do his part for the community in which he lives. Lincoln laid the foundation for his own success when he discovered the power and opportunity of American citizenship.

Lincoln was twenty-three years of age when he found his birthright and entered into the full privileges of citizenship by attending the public meetings in the little town of New Salem, and expressing his opinion and power by voice and ballot.

"I may be wrong in regard to any or all of them," he said, "but, holding it a sound maxim that it is better only some time to be right than at all times to be wrong, so as soon as I discover my opinions to be erroneous I shall be ready to renounce them." His townspeople made him their candidate for the state legislature, and, in accepting their leadership, he declared: "My greatest ambition is to be truly esteemed of my fellow-men by rendering myself worthy of their esteem. I was born and have ever remained in the most humble walks of life. If the good people in their wisdom shall see fit to keep me in the background, I have been too familiar with disappointments to be very much chagrined."

This was the beginning of his political career—and it began with defeat, for, having no acquaintance outside of the village, the residents from the other towns in the county jeered and asked: "Who is this Abraham Lincoln?" and the only response was ridicule and laughter at the sight of the gawky youth with his tan brogans and blue yarn socks.

As a country merchant, he failed and was left $1,100 in debt, and for years afterwards gave his creditors every dollar that he could earn above the cost of living. "That debt," he said in later years, "was the greatest obstacle I have ever met in life. It was my national debt!"

"I will succeed now, anyway," he declared. During the hours after the hard labor of the day, he pored over the law books which he borrowed by walking twenty miles to Springfield and back. At night he would go to the cooper's shop and build a fire of shavings and read by its light. Whenever he gained a new point in law he would put it into practice by drawing up the legal papers for the neighbors. It is such a man as this, with courage to start life again with the future mortgaged, who wins!

THE COURAGE OF CONVICTION—MANHOOD

FAILURE *is but the closed door to success*—try again and you may open it. There is not one man in a thousand who succeeds the first time. We learn only by experience. No matter how many times you have failed, the possibility for success is only greater the next time. It is not defeat that is dishonorable; it is giving up. Struggling to regain his lost foothold, Lincoln, at twenty-four years of age, earned by his honesty the postmastership at New Salem. The mails came but once or twice a week, and in the winter only once a month; the cheapest postage was six cents for thirty miles, and rose as high as twenty-five cents on a letter, according to the distance. The frontiersmen lived largely on credit and did not pay cash even for their letters, so that the postmaster had to carry the accounts. So humble was this political office that Lincoln found it necessary to continue as a day laborer, and he took up surveying to add to his income, so that he might pay off the indebtedness of his failure in business. The foreclosure of a note given by him during his financial reverses resulted in the seizure of his horse, saddle and bridle, including his surveying instruments, leaving him again stripped of all the belongings he had in the world. The keenness of this humiliation wrote itself deep into his character. But his faith in man and in himself never wavered, and during the next election he again accepted the nomination for the legislature—and won.

Lincoln was now twenty-five years of age, and so poor that he had to borrow the money with which to buy suitable clothes to take his seat in the State Capitol at Springfield. No man has ever come into American politics under more adverse conditions. Here was a young legislator who had never lived in a town, who had never lived where there was a church, who had attended school hardly more than six months of his life, and whose entire income was not averaging $4.00 a week. It is this first impulse of political power that tests the character of a man. The temptation of joining the majority and stepping into immediate influence beset Lincoln in the same way that it lures the man of today. True to himself, and to those whom he loved, he took up the cause of the common people, creating a furor by agitating the emancipation of women from political thraldom, raising his his voice for freedom in a moral protest against slavery, and denouncing the citizenship that orders its politics according to personal rewards. He had reached the position in life where he had the courage of his convictions —and that is *Manhood*.

The Portrait Life of Lincoln

PART II

A Photographic Narrative Which Interprets
the Character and Life of
Abraham Lincoln, the Greatest American

THE FOUNDATION OF LINCOLN'S CHARACTER

THERE *comes a moment in every man's life* when he discovers himself; when he finds that the years of labor and experience have laid a foundation upon which he must stand, and that foundation is either strong or weak according to the manner in which he has built it. We are today only what we made ourselves yesterday.

Lincoln was thirty-three years of age when he discovered his fixed position in life. And what a foundation he had laid! Built without tools or material, crude blocks of opportunity,—he found himself standing before the burning heart of humanity, from which there is no turning back. Behind him were those long years of poverty and struggle, the Kentucky cabin, the savage wilds of Indiana, the prairies of Illinois; childhood of poverty, boyhood of toil, the wrestle with destiny. The people had claimed him as their own, and for the first time in his life he could now look straight ahead into the future. A youth of twenty-five years, he had been sent by his townspeople to represent them in the legislature of Illinois, and had allied himself with the cause of the downtrodden. The call of the larger town appealed to him. In his twenty-ninth year, he mounted a borrowed horse, and with all his worldly possessions in the saddlebags, rode away to Springfield to become a lawyer. Here he was again forced to fight his way through many misfortunes, but during his years in the halls of legislation he had made the acquaintance of men who were to become the nation's leaders.

It was here that Lincoln took his first stand against slavery, with but one member of the legislature in sympathy with him. His honesty and integrity at the bar brought him a law practice that allowed him to remove the indebtedness of his earlier life, and at thirty-three years of age he was maintaining himself through his own abilities. He had been eight years a legislator and had risen to the leadership of the Whig party, rejecting the nomination for the governorship. The fortunes of politics are as varied as those of war; when Lincoln first announced his ambition to be sent to Washington as a congressman, the honor was refused him by his party.

Struggle chisels its lines on the countenance of a man. Upon Lincoln's face there was now being written the story that was to become a nation's history. And as he sat for his first photograph, when the call of the people demanded the privilege of looking upon the features of the young lawyer who desired to carry their interests into the halls of congress, he realized that he no longer belonged to himself, but was now a servant of the great democracy. It was the face of prophecy.

FIRST PORTRAIT OF LINCOLN TAKEN WHEN HE ENTERED
NATIONAL POLITICS—AGE 37

This daguerreotype is undoubtedly the first time that Lincoln sat for
his portrait. It was taken during his campaign for Congress
or shortly after his election, when he delivered his first
speeches—from 1846 to 1848. Photograph from
original daguerreotype in possession of
Honorable Robert T. Lincoln
of Chicago, Illinois

THE INFLUENCE OF LOVE ON LINCOLN'S LIFE

THERE is no man so strong that he cannot be won by gentleness. The power of affection is the most subtle force in the world, and interwoven in the lives of all men, whether they be among the greatest or the most humble runs the silken thread of a woman's heart. It was this new world of tenderness that flooded its golden light on Lincoln and ignited new fires of ambition within him. It was when he first entered politics that he first felt the power of a woman's influence. The beauty and the character of little Anne Rutledge, daughter of the village tavernkeeper at New Salem, appealed to Lincoln, but while she admired his manliness and ambition she was betrothed to another. Her companionship with Lincoln is one of the love idylls in American history. The impress which it made upon his character lived with him throughout his life, for in it was written a tragedy. Lincoln's strong friendship for the girl finally won her heart, but in the midst of almost the first happiness which he had ever known his sweetheart fell sick and died. Lincoln was constantly with her during her last hours, and the last song that she sang was for him. The veil of darkness fell upon him, and in all the stirring events that beset his after life he never fully emerged from the melancholy, although her memory was one of his richest possessions. His grief for the dead girl was such that his friends feared that he was losing his mind.

The experience of Lincoln was not unlike that of many others who have saved themselves at such critical moments by summoning their will power to lift them from despair. Work is man's greatest friend. It has been the salvation of man since the world began. Lincoln turned to it in his time of need and entered earnestly into the political problems that were gathering like foreboding clouds over the nation, ardently supporting the moral principles that underly every public question of moment.

It was during these days in his yearning for companionship that he met and married Mary Todd, a Kentucky society girl, whose keen intuition saw in the poor and awkward young legislator a great political destiny. It was a turning point in his career, that fourth day in November in 1842, when this son of the woods, now thirty-three years of age, brought into his life this daughter of pride and social ambition, descended from governors and generals, who, then twenty-one years of age, exclaimed: "I mean to to make him President of the United States. You will see that, as I always told you, I will be the President's wife." Woman became in the life of Lincoln, as she is in the homes of the nation today, the power behind the throne.

PHOTOGRAPH OF MARY TODD, WHO MARRIED ABRAHAM LINCOLN IN 1842

Lincoln was now 33 years of age. This negative was taken some years later at the time
of Lincoln's inauguration for the Presidency, and presents her
in the gown worn at the Inaugural Ball

Original Life Negative in Collection of Americana—Owned
by Mr. Frederick H. Meserve of New York

THE POLITICAL PRINCIPLES OF LINCOLN

AMBITION is a noble comrade, but a dangerous master. It walks beside a man as a faithful friend, but when once given the reins of control it becomes a despot.

Lincoln's mastery of himself was his greatest safeguard in life. He never allowed his political aspirations to overcome his principles, and, while this for a time retarded his progress, it ultimately proved to be the stepping stone upon which he rose to the fullest heights of ambition. He was forced to overcome the same difficulties that beset every man who enters politics. The party leaders, who were unable to mold him according to their desires, gave him but little consideration. This reason which keeps so many men out of politics is in reality the very reason why they should enter them. Strong men of honest purpose need never fear the ultimate outcome of their contest with corruption.

Lincoln's failure to secure the nomination for congress only strengthened his resolution, and on the following election he swept his district by the largest majority that ever had been given to a Whig candidate. The tall, gaunt figure of the young congressman of Illinois, on the streets of Washington, amused the passers-by as he walked to and from the National Capitol; his books tied in a bandana handkerchief, hanging on the end of a cane over his shoulder. While he was considered droll, he did not make a very deep impress on the statesmen of the times, owing largely to the fact that his viewpoint was seldom political or economic, but almost wholly moral. The war with Mexico, and the victory of the American arms, inspired the American spirit of progress, but Lincoln weighed its issue wholly in the scales of the old precept, "Whatever ye would that men should do to you, do ye even so to them." His speeches, coming when the country was elated with military glory, brought denunciation upon him and cost him his political popularity. Political agreements, similar to those which are still practiced today, deprived him of re-election and he returned to the dingy law office in the back room of a two-story building on the square at Springfield. Upon his retirement to private life it was believed that the untactful country lawyer had passed forever from political memory.

The politicians administered "a decisive blow" to the slavery agitation with the Missouri Compromise, only to learn that the heart of humanity cannot be suppressed, and to witness that unforeseen force, Lincoln, being carried to the leadership of the tremendous economic problem that was soon to make him the supreme figure in American politics.

Photograph taken while Lincoln, age 45, was engaged in the Missouri Compromise in 1854—Original taken in an itinerant gallery in Chicago, for George Schneider, editor of "Staats Zeitung"

Photograph taken in 1856, when Lincoln, age 47, was mentioned for Vice-President in the First Republican National Convention

Print in Collection of Mr. Osborn H. Oldroyd of Washington, D. C.

THE IMPULSE THAT HELD LINCOLN STEADFAST

THE *man who takes the world philosophically* can never be permanently beaten. Lincoln was greatly disappointed when his political party set him aside, but in referring to it, in his life as a country lawyer, he said: "I have always been a fatalist and what is to be, will be, or rather, as Hamlet says, 'There is a divinity that shapes our ends, rough hew them how we will.'"

Lincoln admitted that he was losing interest in politics when the repeal of the Missouri Compromise, "stirred him as he never had been stirred before." It aroused him to such an extent that he again entered the arena and became the candidate for the United States Senate. The abolition movement was beginning to sweep New England. The people began to rally to the new standard by the tens of thousands. A great political party, for the altruistic purpose of equality to all men, was being organized.

Lincoln became one of the first Republicans. The oratory of this strange, serious man seemed to inspire the hopes of the people. They looked upon him in bewilderment as they saw this giant of the woods, in a black alpaca coat, with his sleeves rolled up, hammering away at the institution which he believed to be unjust. His appeal was always one of peace, for in his heart or mind there had not yet been a suggestion of the clash of arms that was to come through his leadership. He recognized that slavery was an established institution and that its property rights were legal and just according to the economic system of the times, but he believed that it was unworthy of the high principles of American self-government and that in the interest of civilization we should dissolve the institution by purchasing the chattels from their owners and extending liberty and freedom to all men, regardless of color or race.

"Our political problem now is, 'can we as a nation continue together permanently—forever—half slave and half free,' the problem is too mighty for me. May God superintend the solution," he remarked prophetically.

The one dominant note in Lincoln's character was hope. He believed that hope was the saving grace in humanity. "Free labor has the inspiration of hope, pure slavery has no hope," he said. "The power of hope upon human exertion and happiness is wonderful." When the Republican party came into existence, Lincoln, now forty-seven years of age, stood on the convention floor and held his hearers spellbound; men cheered and women wept; the audience rose to its feet enmasse. The great populace had found their champion at last in this frontier lawyer.

First photograph of Lincoln circulated throughout the country for campaign
purposes—Taken in Chicago in 1857—Lincoln was now 48 years of age.
Original negative by Alexander Hesler burned in Chicago fire.
Print in Collection of Mr. H. W. Fay of DeKalb, Illinois

Ambrotype taken in 1858, shortly after Lincoln's speech at Galesburg,
Illinois—Print owned by Mr. O. H. Oldroyd of Washington

THE RUGGED HONESTY OF LINCOLN'S HEART

*T*HE *heart of every man is a furnace of smoldering fires,* which, when fanned by inspiration, bursts into flame. It is the man who can rekindle the dormant fire of humanity, and cause it to rise from its own ashes, who becomes the leader of his people. There were hundreds of men in Lincoln's time who were more learned in the law than he; there are thousands today. It is not how much you know, but rather how much you know how to use it.

Lincoln knew more about the heart of man than he did the head. The secret of his success and his greatness was his simple humanity. All the political wisdom and legal knowledge of the great men of the times could not overcome the simple, direct words of his homely philosophy that sank deep into the understanding of every hearer.

Listen—you can hear the resonant tones echoing down through the years from the lips of the tall, gaunt orator: "When the white man governs himself, that is self-government; but when he governs himself and also governs another man, that is more than self-government—that is despotism." "No man is good enough to govern another without that other's consent." "Repeal the Missouri Compromise, repeal all compromise, repeal the Declaration of Independence, repeal all past history, still you cannot repeal human nature."

You can see him as he stands in the halls of the Republican Convention in Illinois. He raises his arms and shouts: "We must make this a land of liberty, in fact as it is in name." "We will say to the Southern disunionists, we won't go out of the Union, and you shan't!" You can see that great audience rise to its feet, and as the crowd takes up the slogan, the hall rings with the words that have ignited the hearts of his hearers and set them aflame. Twenty days later, the delegates met in the first National Republican Convention in the city of Philadelphia. Abraham Lincoln received one hundred and ten votes for the Vice-Presidency. It was the following noon that he walked into the tavern in the village where he was trying a law case on the Illinois circuit. He found an excited group discussing the news which had just arrived. The country lawyer carelessly replied that there was another Lincoln up in Massachusetts and it probably meant him. The vote for Lincoln was not sufficient to place his name on the first Republican ticket, but it saved him from the necessity of going down to political oblivion in the election that followed. This is another instance in a man's life where defeat is good fortune.

Lincoln sat for this photograph in Springfield, Illinois, during the
memorable campaign of 1858—age 49 years—Print owned
by Mrs. Harriet Chapman of Charleston, Illinois

Ambrotype taken at Pittsfield, Illinois, October 1, 1858, immediately after
Lincoln had made his speech on the public square—age 49—Original
by C. Jackson, owned by Miss Hattie Gilmer of Pittsfield, Illinois.
Print in collection of Frederick H. Meserve, New York

THE MAN WHO FIRST MADE LINCOLN KNOWN

T O a strong man opposition is a challenge that goads him on to victory. It requires some crucial effort in a man's life to bring out his full strength. We all have what we consider our obstacles in the way of success. The strong man does not attempt to go around them, he cuts straight through them.

Lincoln's life was filled with obstacles, but the last and greatest of them was a man of political strength even greater than his own; a man, who, like himself, had come to the wilderness to fight his way to success—the "Little Giant," Stephen A. Douglas.

You possibly can remember in your own experience some one individual who has had more effect upon your life than all the others that you have ever known. Friends are frequently milestones and occasionally one of them is a turning point.

Douglas was this and more to Lincoln. The roads of the two men had been similar in early life. Douglas knew the school of hard work and poverty, for he had come from the hills of Vermont to the Western plains with but thirty-seven cents in his pocket. He had worked on a farm and taught school. He first appeared in Lincoln's life as a suitor for the hand of the same woman. In this first conflict Lincoln won. They both studied law; they both entered politics; they both entered the legislative halls.

Here their roads seemed to part. Douglas, allying himself with Democratic powers, plunged ahead toward the goal of his ambition. He became Secretary of State in Illinois, and Judge of the Supreme Court; he was sent to Washington as a Congressman; he was elected to the United States Senate. The name of Douglas stood for statesmanship; his strong hand could be seen in all the great political movements; he favored the acquisition of new territory to extend the principles of American self-government; he advocated the compromise of 1850; he formulated the doctrine of Popular Sovereignty, and the famous Kansas-Nebraska Bill.

In this heyday of fame he had almost forgotten the country lawyer back on the Illinois circuit, who had been left so far behind. It did not occur to him that this gaunt youth was now literally walking on his shadow, until suddenly he turned about and found himself once more looking into the strong, homely face of his first opponent—Abraham Lincoln.

The "Little Giant's" career was now brought to a halt for the first time; not by a man who wished to obstruct him, but by one who heard the cry of humanity ahead, and challenged him for the right of way.

PHOTOGRAPH OF STEPHEN A. DOUGLAS TAKEN DURING HIS DEBATES WITH LINCOLN IN 1858

Lincoln was now 49 years of age; Douglas was 45 years—This negative was taken after Douglas
defeated Lincoln for the United States Senate, which was followed two years later
by Lincoln's defeat of Douglas for President of United States

Original in the Collection of American Celebrities—Owned
by Mr. L. C. Handy of Washington, D. C.

THE CHALLENGE THAT TESTED LINCOLN'S STRENGTH

*N*EARLY *every man must be weighed in the balance sooner or later,* but it is not often that the scales of justice are to be the crucial test. Lincoln knew when he challenged Douglas for his seat in the United States Senate that he was challenging destiny, that he was inviting an irrepressible conflict in which both his life and his nation were at stake.

The problem of Slavery, which had been suppressed by politicians for a generation, now demanded the judgment of the American people. Lincoln, now forty-nine years of age, brought it to its first crisis.

"I know there is a God, and He hates injustice and slavery. I see the storm coming. I know His hand is in it. If He has a place and work for me—and I think He has—I believe I am ready. I am nothing, but truth is everything."

Like every man who undertakes to follow his conscience at the risk of his material gain, Lincoln was advised by his friends that he was ruining himself and his party; that he was not only unwise, but a fool; that while he was only a country lawyer, without money, and struggling to make a living, he was courting destruction at the hands of the strongest political leader of the day; a man who was now of independent fortune, whose home in Washington was the gathering place of the distinguished men of the world, and who had been honored in the capitals of Europe.

Lincoln fully realized the difference between himself and his opponent. "With me," he said sadly, "the race of ambition has been a failure—a flat failure; with him it has been one of splendid success." "I affect no contempt for the high eminence he has reached. So reached that the oppressed of my species might have shared with me in the elevation, I would rather stand on that eminence than wear the richest crown that ever pressed a monarch's brow." "I shall try to conduct myself as a gentleman in substance at least, if not in outward polish. The latter I shall never be, but that which constitutes the inside of a gentleman, I hope I understand."

With full conviction of this inequality, Lincoln declared: "We have to fight this battle upon principle, and principle alone." It was now that he sounded the trumpet call to patriotism: "A house divided against itself cannot stand." "I believe this government cannot endure permanently half slave and half free. I do not expect the union to be dissolved—I do not expect the house to fall—but I do expect that it will cease to be divided. It will become all one thing, or all the other."

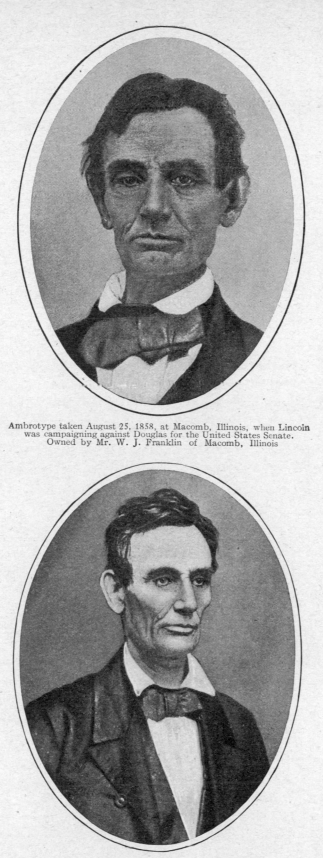

Ambrotype taken August 25, 1858, at Macomb, Illinois, when Lincoln
was campaigning against Douglas for the United States Senate.
Owned by Mr. W. J. Franklin of Macomb, Illinois

Lincoln as he appeared in the political campaign in 1858—age 49—
Original negative owned by Dr. McWilliams of Dwight, Illinois.
Print in possession of Mr. Stuart Brown of Springfield

THE DEFEAT THAT MADE LINCOLN FAMOUS

*T*HE *man who dares to fight a superior foe has already won half the battle.* When Lincoln stepped to the platform to stand beside Douglas, in his first great combat against brilliancy and wit, on that twenty-first day of August, in 1858, he stepped into greatness. Carloads of people from Chicago poured into the little villages of Illinois; the roads were filled with country folk, camping on the prairie, like an army in bivouac.

Douglas journeyed in state in a private car, from which floated the militant strains of a band playing the national airs; a cannon mounted on a flat car proclaimed his coming. Lincoln made his way from town to town by horse or foot, by slow trains or in the caboose of a freight.

Look at the two men as they stand before the cheering multitudes, the champions of the two greatest causes that have ever met in conflict in the annals of mankind—freedom and slavery. There stands Douglas, the "Little Giant," five feet four inches tall; his shoulders broad, his head massive and majestic. There stands Lincoln, his awkward figure, of six feet four inches, slightly stooped; his hair disheveled; his clothes uncouth; his sunken face furrowed by struggle. The throng is cheering and jeering. The strains of "Columbia, the Gem of the Ocean," swell from ten thousand throats. The flags of the Republic flutter in the breeze.

The multitude becomes quiet. A deep, manly voice hushes them to silence: "I don't care whether slavery be voted up or voted down. I don't believe the negro is any kin of mine at all. Who among you expects to live, or have his children live, until slavery be established in Illinois or abolished in South Carolina?" It is the voice of Douglas, combative, forceful, decisive.

The tall, gaunt figure now rises before the multitude. His lips part. "Is slavery wrong? It is the eternal struggle between these two principles—right and wrong—throughout the world. They are two principles that have stood face to face from the beginning of time; and will ever continue to struggle. The one is the common right of humanity, and the other the divine right of kings." It is the voice of Lincoln, resonant, gentle, appealing.

The battle of human emotions rose and fell before seven vast audiences on the circuit of Illinois, with intense heat and fury. Then came the voice of the people—the ballot—the highest law in the land, in whose judgment there speaks an authority which no monarch in the world can overrule— and Lincoln lost.

Faded ambrotype of Lincoln in linen coat, during Douglas debates
at Beardstown, Illinois, in 1858—Original now in Lincoln Monument Collection at Springfield, Illinois—Print in possession
of Mr. Osborn H. Oldroyd of Washington, D. C.

Photograph taken during the famous Lincoln-Douglas debates in
1858— age 49—Collection of Mr. J. C. Browne of Philadelphia

THE APPEAL OF HUMANITY THAT LINCOLN HEARD

THE *world loves a man who knows how to lose.* No man has ever yet gone through life without having to take his losses. That is one of the first lessons that we have to learn—and one of the severest. Abraham Lincoln probably had more setbacks than any man who reads these lines.

While Lincoln was walking home in the rain after his defeat for the United States Senate, he stumbled in the muddy street, but quickly regaining his balance, he naively muttered, "It is a slip and not a fall." The defeat had cost Lincoln nearly a thousand dollars—all the money that he possessed, and the loss of over six months from his law practice. He was left without money for even household expenses. It had cost Douglas eighty thousand dollars of his private fortune to save his seat in the United States Senate and to discover a new political power that was to rival him for the leadership of the American people.

"Though I now sink out of view and shall be forgotten," remarked Lincoln, "I believe I have made some marks which will tell for civil liberty long after I am gone." "Let the past as nothing be. The fight must go on, and I shall fight in the ranks."

Lincoln returned to his work on the circuit to get a living. He carried his love for humanity into the court room and in defense of the fallen appealed to the forgiving spirit of brotherly love. His practice of law was almost wholly based on these principles.

There is an old saying that the truth never dies, and so it was with Lincoln's words. The fires that he had kindled in his campaign were spreading throughout the country. There came loud calls for him from distant cities. He found that his defeat was once again a victory, the stepping stone upon which he was to rise to greater heights.

"This is a world of compensation," was the message that he sent to New England, "He who would be no slave must be content to have no slave. Those who deny freedom to others deserve it not for themselves, and, under a just God, cannot long retain it."

These messages stirred the populace as had nothing else since the Declaration of Independence. His speeches were printed and given wide circulation. His neighbors gazed wonderingly on the growing fame of their townsman, who, to them, was but a simple, uncouth man who had no special position among them. It is the old story of the prophet being without honor in his own home.

LINCOLN AT THE TIME OF JOHN BROWN'S RAID AT HARPER'S FERRY—AGE 50

This negative, taken in 1859, was destroyed in the Chicago Fire—Mrs. Lincoln considered it the best likeness of her husband that she had ever seen—It presents Lincoln as he appeared just before his nomination for the Presidency

Original negative by S. M. Fassett of Chicago, Illinois
Photograph owned by Mr. William Lloyd Garrison of Boston, Massachusetts
Print in collection of Mr. H. W. Fay of DeKalb, Illinois

THE FIRST TEST OF LINCOLN'S NATIONAL GREATNESS

EVERY day that a man lives he is building a reputation—good or bad. There is sure to come a time when this reputation must be weighed in the balance of public opinion. In such an hour as this money may be the most worthless thing in the world. Lincoln, at fifty-one years of age, was still poor in money, but becoming very rich in reputation.

When the call came for him to speak in the metropolis of New York, he knew that the greatest test of his life had now come; that he was now to be measured by the standards of the cosmopolitan world.

A great crowd gathered at Cooper Institute, on that memorable night, the twenty-seventh of February, in 1860. No man since the days of Clay and Webster had spoken to a larger assemblage of intellect. On the platform were the dignitaries of the day. There was William Cullen Bryant, Horace Greeley, and David Dudley Field.

The tall, awkward figure of Lincoln rose from his chair. His hair was disheveled; his coat was too large; his arms hung ungainly at his sides, much longer than his sleeves; and one of the legs of his trousers was two inches above his shoes. The vast audience smiled.

Lincoln, for the first time in his life, seemed to be embarrassed. His hands were trembling. His words were first low and stammering. He had read but three pages and was passing to the fourth when he lost his place. For a moment he hesitated. Then turning the manuscript over two or three times, he threw it upon the table. His shoulders straightened. His whole being seemed to be marshalling power. As he advanced toward the audience, he seemed to grow in stature and might. His face flashed with a glow of inspiration. The words rang through the great amphitheatre as he quoted from Frederick Douglass: "It is written in the sky of America that the slaves shall some day be free."

The audience listened spellbound to his wisdom as he laid before them the entire constitutional and legislative history of the institution of slavery since the nation was founded.

"Neither let us be slandered from our duty by false accusations against us, nor frightened from it by menaces of destruction to the Government nor of dungeons to ourselves. Let us have faith that right makes might, and in that faith, let us, to the end, dare to do our duty as we understand it." No man had ever made such an impression in his first appeal to a New York audience. Lincoln loomed before the nation as the master of men.

Photograph of Lincoln taken in 1860 at the time of his "Cooper Institute Speech" in New York during his campaign for the Presidency—age 51. Original negative by Mathew Brady of New York— Collection of Mr. L. C. Handy of Washington, D. C.

Photograph taken in summer of 1860 for campaign purposes—Original negative owned by Mr. M. C. Tuttle of St. Paul, Minnesota—Print from collection of Mr. Daniel Fish of Minneapolis, Minnesota

THE INSPIRATION OF LINCOLN'S PATRIOTISM

THERE is nothing in this world that merely happens as a matter of chance. Life is filled with surprises as well as disappointments, but back of each one of them is a well-defined cause. The conditions that were now gathering about Lincoln, at fifty-one years of age, were the cumulative results of a long life of work and faith.

The distant rumbles of the greatest political campaign the American people have ever waged, could now be heard. Public opinion was now hopelessly divided over slavery. In the great "Wigwam" at Chicago, the Republicans gathered to nominate the standard bearer. Trains from the East brought the great political organizers of the day, and poured their martial bands and drilled clubs into the dusty streets, only to be met by the tremendous onslaught of enthusiasm that inspired the West.

It was now the day for nominations. The great "Wigwam" was a surging sea of men.

"I nominate William H. Seward, of New York, for President," shouted the clear, penetrating voice of the campaign leader from the East. The name of the great statesman was greeted by a storm of applause.

"I nominate Abraham Lincoln, of Illinois, for President of the United States." The words came from the deep, powerful voice of a Westerner. A tremendous cheer broke from ten thousand throats. The balloting began. Nine states of the South did not respond and the silence was greeted with hisses and jeers. The delegates from the East rose en masse from their seats. Seward had received 173½ votes against 102 for Lincoln—but he was short more than a score necessary for a majority. The balloting proceeded again. Once more the East broke into applause, but from the throats of the West there came a challenging ovation. Seward still led with 184½ votes, but Lincoln had received 181—and still no majority. The third ballot proceeded. A deep suspense fell upon the multitude. Lincoln had received 231½ votes; Seward 180—still 1½ votes short of a majority. The "Wigwam" was in deathlike silence. Suddenly the figure of a man sprang to a chair. "Ohio changes its four votes to Abraham Lincoln!" he shouted. The tumult that rose in that auditorium had never before been witnessed in American politics. A deafening roar echoed across the "Wigwam." The multitude was thrown into pandemonium. Men embraced each other and wept. The crowds at the doors took up the chorus, which echoed through the streets until it was heard a mile away. Abraham Lincoln, the quaint, ungainly prophet of the New West, had been nominated for President of the United States.

Photograph taken before the Republican National Convention at Chicago in 1860—Found in Collection of the late Mr. J. Henry Brown of Philadelphia

Photograph taken at his home in Springfield, Illinois, immediately after his nomination for Presidency in 1860—age 51—Original by Alexander Hesler of Chicago, destroyed during the fire—Print in collection of Mr. Herbert W. Fay of DeKalb, Illinois

THE GATHERING OF HUMANITY UNDER LINCOLN

IF you want to discover just what there is in a man—give him power. It will either make him or wreck him. Prosperity has ruined more men than poverty. Watch a man when he catches his first glow of success and you will discover just how big or how little he really is.

Lincoln was standing in the door of a shop in Springfield, talking, when a shout went up from a group in front of the telegraph office. An excited boy ran across the square shouting, "Mr. Lincoln, Mr. Lincoln, you are nominated!" His townspeople flocked about him, half laughing, half crying. He stood for a moment looking at them curiously. Then he quietly remarked: "My friends, I am glad to receive your congratulations, and as there is a little woman down on Eighth Street who will be glad to hear the news, you must excuse me until I inform her.'

When the delegation from the national convention arrived at the Lincoln home to officially notify him of his nomination, they found a plain two-storied house, with not more than a dozen citizens gathered in front and one of Lincoln's sons perched on the gatepost. Mr. Lincoln was standing in front of the fireplace, his eyes downcast.

The campaign opened with the true Western spirit. Orators stumped the country from one end to the other. Torchlight processions marched through the streets. Campaign songs both ridiculed and eulogized "Honest Abe of the West"—the plain man of the people. The opposing journals jeered at him as a "third rate country lawyer," coarse and clumsy, who could not even speak good grammar. The patriotic press held him before the people as "a man who, by his own genius and force of character, has raised himself from being a penniless, uneducated flatboatman."

The West was exuberant. Seventy thousand excursionists poured into Springfield on a single day to shake the hand of "Our Lincoln." Every road leading to the prairie city was crowded for twenty miles—men, women and children. They brought their tents, camp kettles, and coffee pots. It was a pageant, such as no other American had ever known. The strains of the campaign songs passed along the country roads like trumpet notes. "Our Lincoln is the man! Our Lincoln is the man!"

"Who is this huckster in politics?" demanded a New Englander. "Who is this country court advocate?" Lincoln, without resentment and without humility, calmly replied that his life presented nothing but "the short and simple annals of the poor."

Photograph taken at Springfield, Illinois, in June, 1860—Print
owned by Mr. George B. Ayres—Copyrighted 1894

Ambrotype taken at Springfield, Illinois, May 20, 1860—Original
presented to Governor Marcus L. Ward of New Jersey—Now in
possession of the Ward family of Newark, New Jersey

THE BURDEN OF A NATION ON LINCOLN'S HEART

A MAN'S *life is much like a pendulum.* It swings back and forth over the sweep of events between his birth and death. There is seldom a moment that becomes forever lost. His deeds are ever recurrent. The beat of time in Lincoln's life always brought him before the strong, manly presence of one man. It was this man who now challenged him for the Presidency of the United States—Douglas.

The two were now arrayed against each other in their last great conflict. Douglas, as the candidate of the Northern Democracy, stood for state rights; a principle by which each commonwealth or territory could accept or reject slavery according to its own dictates without interference of Congress or the neighboring states. Lincoln, the candidate of the new Republicanism, placed the responsibility of the problem on Congress as the final authority, declaring that there was no power that legalized slavery anywhere, but that it was within the privilege of Congress to prohibit it in any and every Federal territory. Breckenridge, the candidate of the Southern Democracy, upheld the principle that the citizen of any state has a right to migrate to any territory, taking with him his property by the law of his own state, and that Congress is bound to protect him.

Election day fell on the 6th of November, in 1860. Lincoln came down to his room at the State House, at eight o'clock in the morning. He went to the polls in the late afternoon, and cutting his own name from the head of the Republican ticket, cast the ballot.

The election returns began to arrive in the evening. Lincoln and his friends withdrew to the little telegraph office on the village square. Late in the night the announcement came that his own townspeople had given him a majority. It was then that he showed his first emotion. Cannon boomed from the village green. The villagers remained up until daylight shouting and singing.

It was shortly after midnight that Lincoln was informed of his election. "Boys," he said, "I think I will go home now, for there is a little woman there who would like to hear the news." Three rousing cheers followed him as he passed out into the night. As he entered his bedroom he found his wife had fallen asleep. He touched her gently on the shoulder. "Mary!" She made no answer. He spoke again, a little louder: "Mary, Mary! We are elected!"

The cheers of his townspeople rang through the night, but on his heart there now rested the burden of the nation.

Lincoln as he entered campaign for Presidency at 51 years of age.
Original negative taken in June, 1860, at Springfield, Illinois.
Print owned by Mr. George B. Ayres—Copyright 1881

Ambrotype taken August, 1860, when seventy thousand Westerners
visited Lincoln at his home in Springfield, Illinois—Age 51 years

Original in collection of Mr. William H. Lambert of Philadelphia

THE AFFECTION OF LINCOLN FOR HIS HOME

THERE is no pinnacle of greatness so high that you cannot reach down and touch hands with those at the bottom. When Lincoln realized that he had been lifted to the highest honor within the gift of the American people, he found that humanity was struggling at his feet. He found that while he had secured the required majority in the electoral college, ten states of the South had not cast a ballot for him; that while he had received the votes of 1,866,452 Americans who were opposed to slavery, an army nearly a million greater had cast their ballots against him, for the combined votes of the other candidates reached 2,814,741.

The fearful import of it all cast its shadow upon his face. The cotton states of the South refused to abide by the election. Trade was paralyzed, banks suspended, and the national treasury was nearly bankrupt. The states in the South began to secede. The North became bewildered at the grim forebodings of the end of the republic. Mobs in Boston rose against the abolition agitators, charging them with bringing on the disaster.

The gentle, peace-loving man, about whom the storms were brewing, remained silent. His heart turned to the old log cabin days and to the simple woman, who, as his step-mother, had come into the desolation of his boyhood. It was a long drive through the country, and the river was filled with running ice, but he made the dangerous passage and arrived at the woman's humble cottage. Tears came to their eyes, as she embraced him with deep emotion. "Good bye, Abraham," she said, "I know I shall never see you again. I know your enemies will kill you."

The tall, sad-faced man caressed her and said gently: "No, no, mother; they will not do that. Trust in the Lord and all will be well."

Then, going to the unmarked and neglected grave of his father, he stood over it in reverie, and asked that a suitable tombstone be erected.

It was now his last day in Springfield. He went to the old law office in the little back room, and, stretching himself out on the worn lounge, he lay there a moment with his face toward the ceiling. "Billy," he said, to his law partner, "let the old sign hang there undisturbed. If I live, I'm coming back sometime, and then we'll go right on practicing law as if nothing had ever happened."

Then rising and walking toward the door, he lingered a moment as if to take a last look at the familiar scenes to impress them on his memory, and, turning away, passed down the stairs for the last time.

LINCOLN GREETING HIS NEIGHBORS FOR THE LAST TIME AT HIS OLD HOME

Photograph taken at Springfield, Illinois, in 1861, when Lincoln was bidding
farewell to his townspeople before going to his inauguration at Washington

Negative in the Collection of Americana owned by Mr. F. H. Meserve of New York

CAPITOL AT WASHINGTON WHEN LINCOLN WENT TO HIS INAUGURATION

Photograph taken while the crowd was gathering for the inauguration in 1861, showing the National Capitol of the Republic in course of its construction

Negative in Collection of Americana owned by Mr. Frederick H. Meserve of New York

LINCOLN AT HIS HOME IN SPRINGFIELD—Photograph taken early in 1861 as Lincoln stood with his two younger sons in his front yard—Print in collection of Mr. L. C. Handy of Washington

WHITE HOUSE AS LINCOLN ENTERED IT—Photograph taken at Presidential mansion in Washington, in 1861, in first spring of Lincoln's occupancy—Print in collection of Mr. L. C. Handy of Washington

THE WILLINGNESS OF LINCOLN TO GIVE HIS LIFE

*T*HE *final test of a man's ability is responsibility.* The calm dignity of Lincoln in the storms of violence that were thundering about him perplexed the people. He did not repent of "the crime of having been elected"; he did not ask forgiveness nor apology; neither did he heed the warnings that were flooding upon him from all parts of the country, begging him to resign or to compromise.

The day arrived for him to start for Washington. It was a clear, cold, winter morning—the eleventh of February in 1861. Lincoln rose long before daylight and was at the railroad station at eight o'clock. Less than a hundred people were there to shake hands with him, neighbors who had watched him rise from humbleness to greatness and who knew that the gulf was so narrow that they could clasp hands from either side.

The tall, solemn figure stood on the rear platform of the train that was about to bear him away. The snow was beginning to fall. He raised his hand to silence them, and, baring his head, he looked into their faces. There was a tear on his cheek; his lips quivered. He spoke a few words of encouragement, and bowed: "I bid you an affectionate farewell!" The train pulled away, and as it disappeared from view, Lincoln, the country lawyer, could be seen still lingering on the platform.

At the villages and cities where the train paused, women and children threw bouquets into the car, while men and boys shouted for "Lincoln."

"To the salvation of the Union there needs but one thing," he said, slowly, "the hearts of a people like yours. Of the people when they rise in a mass in behalf of the Union and the liberties of their country, truly may it be said 'the gates of hell cannot prevail against them!'"

For two weeks he passed through the principal cities of the North, leaving words of encouragement and inspiration. It was now Washington's Birthday. He stood at Independence Hall, the historic shrine where the world first heard the Declaration of Independence that proclaimed a new era of civilization in which all men are politically "free and equal."

"If this country cannot be saved without giving up that principle—I would rather be assassinated on this spot than surrender it!" he cried. The words thrilled his hearers. The voice of the solemn man rang through the great gathering: "I have said nothing that I am not willing to live by, and if it be the pleasure of Almighty God,—to die by!"

It was the clear, clarion note of a Nation's patriotism—a man was offering his own life as a sacrifice for the country that he loved.

Photograph taken shortly after Lincoln's election to the Presidency. Believed to be his first portrait with beard, early in 1861, at 52 years of age—Owned by Mr. H. W. Fay, DeKalb, Illinois

Photograph taken at Springfield, Illinois, just prior to Lincoln's departure for Washington in 1861—Original negative by F. M. McNulta—Now owned and copyrighted, 1894, by Mr. Herbert Wells Fay of DeKalb, Illinois

THE FORTITUDE OF LINCOLN IN HOUR OF TRIAL

THE man who stands for a principle must value duty higher than life. When Lincoln was told that it was sworn that he would never enter Washington alive, he determined to die if need be only at the Nation's capital with his hand at the helm of state. He had a work to do—and he intended to do it.

His journey was fraught with danger. There was a hurried conference with a messenger in his room at Harrisburg. A plot had been discovered to take his life. Kissing his wife and children good bye, he left them sobbing and slipped away into the night with two friends.

When Washington awakened on the morning of the twenty-fourth of February, it was startled to find that the new President, Abraham Lincoln, was in their midst; that he had entered the capital of the republic on a midnight train as a common passenger, unknown and unrecognized by his fellow-travelers,—a stranger.

The National capital was in no welcoming mood. It was a Southern slave-holding community and looked upon Lincoln as a revolutionist who intended to set up a new system of government under the radical doctrines of a new republican party, which had come into being to destroy their property rights. The statesmen, who had known slavery as an American institution from the founding of the republic, looked upon the new party as a menace to the Nation and shook their heads in dismay. Here was a man who would upset the republic.

At daybreak on the fourth of March, in 1861, the city of Washington was astir. There was the clatter of cavalry and the tramp of the militia in the streets. The Senate had been in session the whole night long and the drowsy statesmen walked the corridors with sullen faces.

At noon the inaugural procession moved slowly over the historic route which almost every President since Jefferson had traveled to take his oath of office. Thousands of people crowded the streets. Around the presidential carriage rode the protecting guard of militia to thwart any attempt at assassination. Platoons of soldiers were stationed along the avenue. Riflemen were posted on the roof-tops, watching for the slightest sign of hostility, while cavalrymen guarded every approach from the side streets.

As Lincoln entered the Senate chamber, his pale face and black attire brought a stillness over the august body. He was leaning on the arm of an old man withered and bowed with age—President Buchanan, from whom he was now to lift the weight of a crumbling republic.

Photograph of Lincoln taken early in 1861 about the time that he
entered the White House—Original negative by Alexander Hesler
of Chicago—Print owned by Mr. Frank A. Brown of Minneapolis

Photograph of Lincoln taken just before leaving Springfield for the
White House in 1861, age 52 years—Original negative by
C. S. German—Print owned by Mr. Allen Jasper Conant

THE CRUMBLING NATION IN LINCOLN'S ARMS

WHEN *the world thinks that a man has won, his struggles have just begun.* When Lincoln stood before the throng at the steps of the National Capitol, to be inaugurated President of the United States, the first "government of the people, by the people, and for the people," that the world had ever known, he stood as the personification of the principles upon which the republic is founded.

Before him now gathered a remarkable group of men who had made history. Here were statesmen who had served their country through long lives of distinguished loyalty and had seen it rise from the war with England to become one of the world's greatest powers. Here were diplomats of foreign embassies who were pledged to the divine rights of kings and shook their heads prophetically as they agreed that the theory of self-government was now to take its place as the heresy of civilization.

Lincoln rose and stood before them. There was a faint cheer from the crowd that was being held in restraint by the battalion of soldiers. Riflemen scanned the scene from the capitol windows, while just ahead moved a battery of flying artillery.

There was a moment's pause as Lincoln moved forward. He removed his tall silk hat. A short, heavy, strong-featured man stretched forth his hand and took it from him. Lincoln bowed courteously and smiled. It was Stephen A. Douglas, the political antagonist of his whole public career, the man who had fought him through every step of progress, and who had just contested him for the crowning honor of his life—and lost.

"If I can't be President," he whispered to a member of the Lincoln party, "I at least can hold his hat."

As Lincoln stood there, pledging himself to preserve, protect and defend the Constitution and the Union, every ear was strained to catch the words from his lips:

"I am loath to close," he said. "We are not enemies, but friends. We must not be enemies. Though passion may have strained, it must not break our bonds of affection. The mystic chords of memory, stretching from every battlefield and patriot grave to every living heart and hearthstone all over this broad land, will yet swell the chorus of the Union, when again touched, as surely they will be, by the better angels of our nature."

A hush fell over the assemblage. The oath of office came from his lips. The cannons of the battery boomed. And Abraham Lincoln, the son of a log cabin, held the future of a nation in his arms.

LINCOLN AT HIS INAUGURATION—Photograph taken while Lincoln was delivering his inaugural address before the great throng that had gathered at the National Capitol—The judges of the Supreme Court can be seen sitting at his left—Print in the Brady-Gardner Collection deposited at Springfield, Massachusetts.

THE DETERMINED WILL OF LINCOLN AMONG MEN

POWER is not so much what a man can accomplish as what he can lead others to do. Lincoln had the ability to lead men. It was with a heavy heart that he entered the White House. The South had insisted upon the supremacy of the state as the true interpretation of the Constitution, and to uphold this principle seven historic old states had withdrawn and established a new republic to be known as the Confederate States of America.

The Southern Senators and Representatives were withdrawing from the Congress of the United States. The Federal courts were suspending, and the stars and stripes were being hauled down from their flagstaffs. The prophecy of Lincoln had come true and the house was now divided.

Lincoln gathered his cabinet about him. Among them were statesmen who had opposed him for the nomination for the Presidency and who now beheld him with grave perplexity. They were strong men of strong convictions, but they could little comprehend the subtle power of this strange man who had come up from the western wilderness and taken control of their government.

Look at Lincoln as he sat in his cabinet room. Among the faces of those men there is not a friend, not one who had known Lincoln a year before. But to establish the new spirit of republicanism in power, he had gathered about him this cabinet composed of his rivals for political honors and had not even reserved for himself the appointment of one personal friend to whom he might now turn.

There they sat, in their inability to measure the greatness of their chief, contending for leadership and power, only to find at last that a mighty man may come from the rough paths through the woods, one who takes his heart from the oak and his judgment from the mountain rocks.

In the corridors of the White House strode the wily politicians in the wild stampede for office in the new political party that had come into power for the first time. Within—was dissension and misunderstanding, political prowess and manipulation. Without—were the rumbles of discontent and threats of war. But there sat Lincoln, with words of hope and courage, turning away impatience and wrath with pointed stories of wit and philosophy, holding the threads of a nation together with the keen insight of human nature and the instinctive understanding of men, while in his mind he was working out the solution in the mighty problem of maintaining the American people one and inseparable.

Lincoln's Vice-President in 1861-1865
HANNIBAL HAMLIN of Maine

Lincoln's Secretary of War in 1862-1865
EDWIN M. STANTON of Ohio

Lincoln's Secretary of War in 1861-1862
SIMON CAMERON of Pennsylvania

Lincoln's Secretary of State in 1861-1865
WILLIAM H. SEWARD of New York

PHOTOGRAPHS OF MEMBERS OF PRESIDENT LINCOLN'S CABINET

Original negatives taken from 1861-1865 by Mathew Brady of Washington. Now in the Brady-Gardner Collection
of Seven Thousand Negatives deposited at Springfield, Massachusetts

THE TRUE TEST OF LINCOLN'S STATESMANSHIP

*T*HE *man who can control other men* without their realizing it is in himself great. The firm decision of gentleness has won more victories than aggressive force. The statesmen sitting in Lincoln's political family all felt that in experience and judgment they were much greater than their chief; each man was confident that he alone was the real master of the situation. Now they were advising, now threatening, now demanding. Clamor and intrigue surrounded him.

"Let the Union slide," shouted the abolitionists.

"Let the South go her way. The North can take care of itself," cried the financial powers.

"Wayward sisters, depart in peace," exclaimed the venerable patriot of two wars who was now in command of the Federal Army.

Lincoln heard the words but made no reply.

"Turn public attention immediately by waging a war with some foreign nation on some pretext or other and thus force the South to unite with the North to protect themselves against foreign invasion," advised the most distinguished member of the cabinet.

"We must change the question before the public from one upon slavery or about slavery, to one upon union or disunion," he urged. "I would demand explanations (on the Monroe Doctrine) from Spain and France, energetically, at once . . . and if not received . . . I would convene Congress and declare war against them. I would seek explanations from Great Britain and Russia, and send agents into Canada, Mexico, and Central America to arouse a vigorous spirit of continental independence."

But the man in the White House remained calm. He betrayed no emotion of anger against the insinuations nor boastful self-confidence. Whether it was to be war or peace, union or disunion, life or death, he took the fearful burden of it wholly upon his own shoulders, with the simple words that whatever the course might be: "I must do it."

"Remind the British that we have whipped them in two wars," urged the cabinet adviser, "and are ready to fight them again, and, if need be, two or three other European powers at the same time."

Lincoln sat at his cabinet table, with his eyes looking out of the window on the soldiers that guarded the White House, as if peering into the future. "One war at a time," he said, softly. "One war at a time."

Native common sense was now in contest with statesmanship.

Lincoln's Secretary of Treasury in 1861-1864
SALMON P. CHASE of Ohio

Now in the Original Brady Collection
at Springfield, Massachusetts

Lincoln's Secretary of the Navy in 1861-1865
GIDEON WELLES of Connecticut

Now in the Original Brady Collection
at Springfield, Massachusetts

Lincoln's Secretary of the Interior in 1861-1865
CALEB B. SMITH of Indiana

Now in the Original Brady Collection
at Springfield, Massachusetts

Lincoln's Postmaster-General in 1861-1864
MONTGOMERY BLAIR of Maryland

Now in the Collection of Mr. L. C. Handy
at Washington, District of Columbia

PHOTOGRAPHS OF MEMBERS OF PRESIDENT LINCOLN'S CABINET

Original negatives taken from 1861-1865 by Mathew Brady of Washington

THE STRENGTH OF LINCOLN IN A NATION'S PERIL

A MAN must be willing to resign to the inevitable, but he must first be sure that it is the inevitable. Lincoln knew that every stroke of the hour was now moving him toward it; that there was no human power that could resist it. All that he could now do was to meet it with the courage and resignation of manhood.

It was on the twelfth of April in 1861—the day was Friday. Lincoln had arisen with the dawn and was sitting at his morning duties in the executive mansion when a messenger approached.

"They have fired on Fort Sumter!" he exclaimed.

The message startled the National capital and passed from city to city until it had aroused the continent and was echoing around the world. The ancient monarchies well understood its meaning.

The American Flag had been assailed; not by a foreign foe, but by its own sons. The sound of that shot was like the tap of a drum calling its people to arms. The South, inspired by its own convictions, rose in courage and cheered. The North sprang to its guns in an outburst of frenzied patriotism. The bonds of brotherhood were now severed. The whole people cried out for war.

Excited groups of statesmen gathered at the White House. Party dogmas and doctrines were forgotten. Diplomatic relations and policies were set aside. Political enemies clasped hands and pledged themselves to the service of their country.

Lincoln walked among them, grave and calm. All day long came the news of the deadly fire in the ramparts of Fort Sumter. Lincoln shook his head as he listened to the despatches that told of the brave defense of the little garrison, who for thirty-four hours stood at their post, enveloped in sheets of flame, and when they, too, faced the inevitable, marched bravely out on that Sunday afternoon with colors flying and drums beating, saluting the bullet-ridden flag of the Union with fifty guns as it was lowered from its staff.

The Confederate States of America had now proclaimed their empire. The sovereignty of the state had now been baptized by shot and shell. The last vestige of "federal despotism," as they looked upon it, was now driven from their soil and the American people stood arrayed against each other in two mighty republics, ready and waiting to lay down their lives on the fields of battle for the sake of the principles which each held more precious than life. The inevitable had come.

Lincoln's Attorney-General in 1861-1863
EDWARD BATES of Missouri

Now in the Original Brady Collection
at Springfield, Massachusetts

Lincoln's Assistant Secretary of War
CHARLES A. DANA of New York

Now in the Original Brady Collection
at Springfield, Massachusetts

Lincoln's Secretary of the Treasury in 1864-1865
WILLIAM P. FESSENDEN of Maine

Now in the Collection of Mr. L. C. Handy
at Washington, District of Columbia

Lincoln's Secretary of Interior in 1863-1865
JOHN P. USHER of Indiana

Now in the Original Brady Collection
at Springfield, Massachusetts

PHOTOGRAPHS OF MEMBERS OF PRESIDENT LINCOLN'S CABINET

Original negatives taken from 1861-1865 by Mathew Brady of Washington

THE FAITH OF LINCOLN IN THE COMMON PEOPLE

THE heart of the people has never failed to respond when duty calls it—and never will. The great army of humanity that has come down through the ages in endless procession since the world began may have seemed to waver at times under the sieges of fire, but its lines have never been known to break when standing on the battle-line of civilization.

And so it was when Lincoln called for volunteers to defend the nation's flag, and the Confederacy marshaled its sons under the new standard of the Stars and Bars. Throughout the North could be heard the tramp of marching men. Over the green plantations of the South rolled the call to arms. From village to village sounded the drumbeat of the Union. Men left their plows and laid down their tools of labor to take up arms in defense of their homes and their country, while wives and mothers prayed.

The tragedy of it all lay before the eyes of Lincoln. The flag of the Confederacy floated on the bluffs across the Potomac River in Virginia. In the streets before him were women fleeing with their children to the hills. Great wagons of ammunition and provisions thundered over the thoroughfares. Outside, at the door, he could hear the gruff voices of the soldiers barricading his home into a fortress. Office seekers and statesmen walked the corridors of the White House with muskets and revolvers.

Lincoln, turning to his wife and children, urged them to flee from the city in safety. The terror-stricken woman looked into the sad face of her husband, and, clinging to his arm, whispered, "I am as safe as you. I shall never leave you here alone."

It was five o'clock in the evening on the nineteenth of April, in 1861. Lincoln stood at the window in the White House. Far down the street, he could see a great body of men moving nearer and nearer—the men of the North, who had heard his call and had come to the defense of their country,—dusty, torn and bleeding. On their faces was grim determination. Behind them, in single file, came seventeen stretchers bearing the wounded. Their dead they had left hehind in the streets of Baltimore, where, a few hours before, they had shed the first blood for the Union.

On came the volunteers, pouring floods of men into the national capital, until, on the Fourth of July, three hundred thousand were marching under the Stars and Stripes, and from every hill and valley throughout the land echoed the refrain: "We are coming, Father Abraham, three hundred thousand more!"

Lincoln's Secretary of the Treasury in 1865
HUGH MCCULLOCH of Indiana

Now in the Collection of Mr. L. C. Handy
at Washington, District of Columbia

Lincoln's Attorney-General in 1864-1865
JAMES SPEED of Kentucky

Now in the Original Brady Collection
at Springfield, Massachusetts

Lincoln's Postmaster-General in 1864-1865
WILLIAM DENNISON of Ohio

Now in the Collection of Mr. L. C. Handy
at Washington, District of Columbia

Lincoln's Second Vice-President in 1865
ANDREW JOHNSON of North Carolina

Now in the Collection of Mr. L. C. Handy
at Washington, District of Columbia

PHOTOGRAPHS OF MEMBERS OF PRESIDENT LINCOLN'S CABINET

Original negatives taken from 1861-1865 by Mathew Brady of Washington

THE ABILITY OF LINCOLN TO OVERCOME DEFEAT

THERE is one quality that always comes to the aid of a man in time of adversity—it is patience. This has never been demonstrated more forcibly than in the experience of Lincoln during the early days when the American people were in fratricidal war.

Congress authorized an army of a half million men, with a half billion dollars to support it. The Confederacy marshaled its strongest sons to defend its capital at Richmond. The North, with the courage of its great army and wealth, was eager to pit itself against the new republic and appealed to Lincoln to strike the fatal blow. But Lincoln, always with hope in his heart that some unforeseen power would avert the tragedy, waited patiently. The North, in its impatience, charged him with being a coward.

Lincoln listened to the abuse without reply. It was now July—the twenty-first day. The sun rose hot on that Sunday morning. Lincoln went to church. Suddenly the city was aroused. The two great armies were standing face to face at Manassas, but thirty-two miles from Washington. Couriers hurried to the White House. There was deep anxiety on the face of the President. The North and South were in battle. The two great fighting forces were in deadly combat.

"The Union army is victorious!" Crowds waited anxiously for the next word. The dispatches ceased coming. The prolonged silence perplexed the watchers and they were seized with a strange fear.

It was six o'clock in the evening. A statesman hurried to the White House and asked excitedly for Lincoln.

"The battle is lost," he exclaimed. "The Confederates are coming!"

Lincoln quietly turned, and, without a word, went to the War Department. The telegraph instruments were ticking the story of the fearful disaster and the probable capture of Washington. Turning to the door, he returned to the White House, and threw himself onto a lounge.

It was midnight when the routed army staggered across Long Bridge into the city, and when morning dawned the defeated soldiers were pouring into Washington in great streams of frightened humanity.

Lincoln still lay on the lounge. His deep set eyes had not closed during the long night. But beneath them there seemed to brood a new strength. He arose and greeted the disheartened soldiers with the grasp of a warm heart. On his face was a fixed expression of determination— the determination of a man who had learned how to grow strong in defeat.

Photograph of Lincoln seated with his secretaries, Nicolay and Hay—Taken in Springfield, Illinois, in 1861, just before leaving for Washington—Print in the Brady-Gardner Collection at Springfield, Massachusetts

Photograph presented by Lincoln to Mrs. Lucy G. Speed, on October 3, 1861 on which he inscribed his autograph—Negative in the Collection of Americana in possession of Mr. Frederick H. Meserve of New York

THE HOPEFULNESS OF LINCOLN IN MISFORTUNE

A MAN *who spends his time fighting* over old battles is surely lost. Life, in its shortness, gives us no opportunity to re-live the lost days. The only value of yesterday is the experience that we learned from it; otherwise nature would never have given us memory.

Lincoln understood life. Bull Run was nothing more than the price that is paid for experience. His life had been full of Bull Runs, and from every defeat he had gained a great victory.

The wrath of the North now fell upon him. Famine began to lay its hand upon the country. The nation was overwhelmed in debt. The army was costing more than two millions of dollars a day—and yet no battles were being won. Men pressed about him with conflicting advice. Cabinet ministers charged him with incompetency. His friends appealed to him to resign, or to march his armies against the capital of the Confederacy and conquer it by overwhelming numbers.

The generals upon whom he relied, failed to meet the emergencies. The mighty Confederacy strengthened its power of government and slowly but firmly drew its lines more tightly around the nation's capital.

As Lincoln sat surrounded by his family, the battle-line crossed the very threshold of his home. A Southerner by birth, he found many of his dearest friends under the flag of the Confederacy. Mrs. Lincoln's own family were arrayed against the Union. Her sisters were parted from her by the war, and their husbands were fighting against her husband's cause. When the news came of the Union victory at Shiloh, and Mrs. Lincoln found it her duty to receive in honor of the victorious soldiers, one of her own brothers, the darling of her heart, lay dead in a uniform of gray on that battlefield.

Lincoln, with the terrible imprint of it all being written upon his countenance, stood for hours with his big white gloved hand grasping the hands of the passing throng, but his eyes were looking far beyond into the trenches of the humanity that he loved. And when he received the news of the terrible slaughter at Antietam, where, in defense of the nation's capital, the army in blue withstood the army in gray and forced it back on to its own soil, Lincoln, with his heart overflowing with hope in the belief that now the war was to cease, went to the battlefield and looked into the faces of the soldiers upon whom he relied in this hour of need.

LINCOLN IN CAMP WITH THE ARMY AT ANTIETAM

Photograph taken on October 3, 1862, when Lincoln was
standing in front of General McClellan's tent—Taken
by Mathew Brady, Government Photographer

PRESIDENT LINCOLN ON BATTLEFIELD OF ANTIETAM UNDER GUARD OF THE SECRET SERVICE

Original negative taken by Mathew Brady on October 3, 1862—Lincoln was accompanied by Allan Pinkerton
(Major Allen) first chief of the Secret Service, standing at his right, and General McClernand at his left—
Deposited in the Original Collection of seven thousand negatives valued at $150,000 at
Springfield, Massachusetts—Copyright, 1907, by Mr Edward Bailey Eaton

LINCOLN WITH HIS GENERALS—Photograph taken in the army of the Potomac at Antietam, on October 3, 1862, while Lincoln was addressing General McClellan and staff—Negative in Brady-Gardner Collection at Springfield, Massachusetts—Copyright, 1907, by Mr. Edward Bailey Eaton

LINCOLN WITH HIS SOLDIERS AT THE BATTLE-LINE—Photograph taken while Lincoln was inspecting conditions in army at Antietam on October 3, 1862—Original negative by Mathew Brady—Print in Collection of Mr. C. M. Derickson of Monessen, Pennsylvania

President Lincoln in General McClellan's Tent at Battle Grounds of Antietam

Original negative taken by Mathew Brady on October 3, 1862, while Lincoln was in conference
with General McClellan a few days after the great battle—Now deposited in the
Brady-Gardner Collection at Springfield, Massachusetts—Copyright, 1907,
by Mr. Edward Bailey Eaton and valued at ten thousand dollars

PRESIDENT LINCOLN IN THE SECOND YEAR OF THE AMERICAN CIVIL WAR

Original negative taken by Mathew Brady in Washington, in 1862
Print owned by Mr. Baldwin Coolidge of Boston, Massachusetts

THE MIGHT OF LINCOLN IN HIS COUNTRY'S CRISIS

IN every man's life there are times when the burdens that press upon him are beyond all human endurance; when patience is no longer a virtue, and all the powers within him demand decision and action. Lincoln found that there was a moment when even sympathy and diplomacy must give way to the destiny of mankind; when it must work out its own salvation or destruction with the blood of men.

It was five days after the battle of Antietam—the twenty-second day of September in 1862. Members of the cabinet were seated in secret session. Lincoln sat with a book in his hands. The faces of the statesmen were stern. He did not seem to notice them as they entered. Then, turning to them, he said: "Gentlemen, did you ever read anything from Artemus Ward? Let me read you a chapter that is very funny."

A look of anger passed over the ministers. Lincoln laughed heartily; not a member of the cabinet smiled.

"Well," he said, "let's have another chapter." He continued to read with great deliberation. The statesmen were astonished. Abruptly, he threw the book down, and exclaimed: "Gentlemen, why don't you laugh? With the fearful strain that is upon me night and day if I do not laugh I shall die, and you need this medicine as much as I do."

His face and his tone became grave. Turning to his tall silk hat that lay upon the table, he took a paper from it. He gazed for a moment at his ministers. "I have called you here," he said slowly, "upon very important business. I have prepared a little paper of much significance . . . I have said nothing to any one, but I have made a promise to myself—and to my Maker. I am now going to fulfill that promise."

Holding the sheets before him, he began to read. His voice was low but firm: "On the first day of January, in the year of our Lord 1863, all persons held as then slaves in any state or designated part of a State, the people whereof shall then be in rebellion against the United States, shall be then, thenceforth and forever free."

The statesmen were silent. The tremendous meaning of it all flooded upon them. The man upon whom they had looked as without power of decision, sat before them with grim determination. In the might of decision, he had with a single blow issued to the world a proclamation that was to break the shackles of bondage and to shake the foundations of civilization.

The news swept through the army. "Lincoln has freed the slaves!" The North shouted in exultation. The South retorted in defiance.

PHOTOGRAPH TAKEN AFTER THE FIRST EMANCIPATION PROCLAMATION

Original negative by Mathew Brady at Washington in September, 1862, age 53 years
Print in possession of Mr. L. C. Handy of Washington, District of Columbia

THE HAND OF LINCOLN ON THE CHAIN OF BONDAGE

THE greatest gift that man has ever known is moral courage. It is the secret power that makes men rise above themselves and rule their destiny. It is a legacy that is bequeathed to every living man to use or not to use according to his own desire. You are your own master of your God-given fortunes and you alone are held accountable for them.

The Confederacy reeled at the blow of the Emancipation Proclamation and referred to it as the "most execrable measure recorded in the history of guilty man." Lincoln understood the responsibility upon him. He saw in it the omen of racial and social strife to come.

"I do it," he said, "only to save the Union . . . I can only trust in God."

It was New Year's Day in 1863. The White House was a scene of social brilliancy. Ministers from foreign nations, senators and congress-men and army officers gathered to pay their respects to the courageous republic. Lincoln stood among them with words of cordial greeting. Passing from them, he entered the executive chamber. He seated himself at the long cabinet table. Before him lay a broad sheet, the words of which were engrossed in heavy letters. He raised his pen, and, dipping it in the ink, moved his hand to the place for the signature. Hesitating a moment, he dropped the pen. Turning toward the cabinet minister, and his son, who were the only persons in the room, he said: "I never, in my life, felt more certain that I was doing right than I do in signing this paper. But I have been shaking hands since nine o'clock this morning, till my arm is stiff and numb. If my name goes into history it will be for this act, and my whole soul is in it. If my hand trembles when I sign this proclamation, they will say: 'He hesitated.' "

Turning again to the table, he took up the pen, and slowly but firmly wrote at the close of the document —"Abraham Lincoln." He sat for a moment with his eyes fixed on the signature. Looking up, he smiled and said: "That will do!"

His hand fell by his side – the hand that by a single stroke had un-chained a race that had been held in bondage almost since the world began. The cabinet member left the room. Lincoln looked straight ahead as though into the future. The lines were chiseled deep about his lips. He seemed to be listening as though he could hear the clanking shackles break from the arms of three million human beings, as though he could hear the anguished sigh that arose from three million human hearts.

PHOTOGRAPH OF LINCOLN SHORTLY AFTER THE SIGNING
OF THE EMANCIPATION PROCLAMATION

Original negative taken by Alexander Gardner at Washington, in 1863, when
Lincoln, age 54, broke the chains that had bound three million slaves

Negative in the Collection of Americana of Frederick H. Meserve, New York

THE GREATEST SACRIFICE OF LINCOLN'S LIFE

E who forgets that he was once a child is not a man. The dearest memories that most of us possess are those of childhood; we look back at those long lost days with fondest recollections. Lincoln never got so far that he could not hear the call of the whip-poor-will and brown thrush singing in those old Kentucky forests far away.

Lincoln loved children. He had three sons, another having died in infancy. The army to him was but somebody's boys—his boys; over two million boys under twenty-one years of age; a million not even eighteen; eight hundred thousand less than seventeen; two hundred thousand had not reached sixteen; while one hundred thousand children less than fifteen years of age were standing on the battle-line under the Stars and Stripes.

It was during the darkest days of the war, that Lincoln was called upon to make his own sacrifice. The White House was the scene of a brilliant reception. The President, with his wife leaning on his arm, entered the room where the dignitaries of the world were gathered to meet him. The notes of the Marine Band floated far away to the chamber where the companion of his heart lay in fever—his twelve-year-old boy, Willie. The night passed slowly. Lincoln left the ball-room and went to the chamber.

"He is not as well tonight," remarked the physician. "He may be better in a few days." The passing hours were filled with messages from the boys who were dying on the field of battle. Lincoln turned again to his own chamber. His head was bowed with grief. He came to the bed, and, lifting the cover from the face of his child, he gazed into it.

"My poor boy," he murmured. "He was too good for this earth. God has called him home. I know he is much better off in heaven, but we loved him so. It is hard hard—to have him die!" Great sobs choked his words. He bowed his head in his hands, and his gaunt frame shook.

Those of you who have lost sons, stand with him here a moment. Listen to the sobs of the broken-hearted mother. Look upon the grief of a father. Bending over her gently, he takes her by the arm and leads her to the window: "Mother, do you see that large, white building on the hill yonder?" He is pointing to the asylum on the hill. "Try to control your grief, for it will drive you mad, and we may have to send you there."

The lifeless body of the beloved boy lay in the green room, beneath his office. Strong men gathered about him, ambassadors, senators and soldiers, all struggling with their tears—for, whatever the dissensions of life may be, this is a moment when all the world has a heart in common.

Photograph of President Lincoln's son, William Wallace
Lincoln, who died at the White House, February 20,
1862, at twelve years of age—Collection of
Mr. Frederick H. Meserve of New York

Photograph of Thomas (Tad) Lincoln, born April 4, 1853,
who became the companion of President Lincoln during
his last years in the White House—The oldest son,
Robert Todd Lincoln, was in Harvard—
Collection of Frederick H. Meserve

THE POWER OF LINCOLN TO CONQUER HIMSELF

GREAT *achievements are but the accumulation of conquered difficulties.* As we look over our own experiences we find that there is one simple truth in life that is always well worth remembering— our richest possessions are those which cost us the most, not in money, but in disappointments, sacrifices, and hope. The Emancipation Proclamation plunged the nation into despair. It was a bugle call to the hosts of the South who now arose in vengeance to strike a staggering blow at the man who had despoiled them of their property.

The mighty columns of the Confederacy were now sweeping toward the North, vowing that they would unfurl their flag over the capitol at Washington and force a prostrate nation to return their property to them. The North, stricken with terror, called for the resignation of Lincoln, the man who was responsible for the disaster, and threatened to take his life.

"I shall never be happy again," he said. "My life springs are wearing out and I shall not last . . . I long ago made up my mind that if anybody wants to kill me, he may do it." Then he added dejectedly, "How hard it is to die, unless I can make the world understand that I would be willing to die if I could be sure I am doing my work toward lifting the burdens from all mankind!"

It was a bright afternoon in May, in 1863. The door leading to the family apartments in the White House swung open. There stood Lincoln, holding a telegram in his hand. It was from Chancellorsville.

"My God! My God!" he cried in broken tones. "What will the country say? Oh, what will the country say?"

He tottered to a chair, and sat down. As the night fell he paced the floor in deep thought. In front of him were heaps of letters, the purport of which he well knew. They were piteous appeals for peace, the cries of heart-stricken mothers. They were denunciations branding him with the blood of the hundred thousand homes that were being left fatherless.

The doors of the room were ajar. The night was warm; its stillness was broken only by the slow, steady tread back and forth. One by one the hours passed, but Lincoln, with head bowed, walked the chamber, the steady footfalls breaking the silence. A battle greater than Chancellorsville was raging within him. When the morning light sifted through the window, Lincoln, his eyes heavy with sleeplessness, sat at his desk, but his face was strong in resignation. A great battle had been fought that night—and Lincoln had won another victory over himself.

Photograph of Lincoln taken at Washington in 1863
shortly after the Battle of Chancellorsville—
Original negative by Mathew Brady

Photograph taken the Sunday before Lincoln left for the
Battlefield of Gettysburg in November, 1863—
Original negative by Mathew Brady

THE HUMILITY OF LINCOLN IN HOUR OF VICTORY

THAT *it is always darkest just before the dawn* is a truth that comes to every man sooner or later. No matter how hard the storm may rage there is always a break in the clouds through which the golden light floods the heart with warmth and hope.

The sun rose hot on the first morning in July, in the year 1863. Its scorching rays looked down on two great armies standing face to face. The legions of the South, on their onward march into the strongholds of the North, stood in battle-line against the hosts in blue under the Stars and Stripes on the field of Gettysburg. Nearly two hundred thousand strong, they passed through the fire of hell for the sake of the cause that they loved. On and on they charged, beneath the maddening hail of iron, into the terrible roar and din of belching flame, their banners flying; and when the clouds of smoke lifted at the end of the third day, more than fifty thousand dead, wounded and missing, had laid down their lives on the altar of sacrifice.

Lincoln, with anxiety and anguish on his face, waited for the tidings. When the news came to him that the flag of the republic had triumphed, that the great army of the Confederacy had been driven from Northern soil and was fleeing back to its own beautiful valley—he thanked God.

It was four months later that Lincoln stood on the battlefield at Gettysburg. Before him was a great throng of people. Garlands of flowers were placed upon the graves of the heroes who had given their lives on the sacred ground on those terrible days in July. The chill of November had now fallen upon the hills.

Dressed in black, the somberness and ghastly pallor of his face brought silence to the multitude. His words, as if by magic, fell upon their ears: "Four score and seven years ago, our fathers brought forth on this continent a new nation, conceived in liberty, and dedicated to the proposition that all men were created equal."

A hush fell over the great audience. There was now and then an outburst of suppressed emotion. The notes rang clear. "It is due our own who have died here . . . This nation in God shall have a new proof of freedom . . . Government of the people, by the people, for the people, shall not perish from the earth."

The tall, solemn figure disappeared from view. As he resumed his seat the words seemed to leap from man to man across the continent until the American people were inflamed by their inspiration, the fires of which are still blazing, and will forever blaze, down through the generations.

Photograph Taken During Lincoln's Speech on the Battlefield of Gettysburg

Original negative by Alexander Gardner on November 19, 1863, while Lincoln was delivering his famous Gettysburg address at the consecration of the cemetery

Original in the Brady-Gardner Collection at Springfield, Massachusetts
Copyrighted, 1910, by the Patriot Publishing Company

Photograph taken about the time of the Battle of Gettysburg
in 1863—Original negative by Mathew Brady

Photograph taken in the Brady gallery at the National Capital
in 1863 during darkest days of Civil War—Original negative
by Mathew Brady—Life negative in Collection of
Americana of Frederick H. Meserve of New York

Photograph taken shortly after Lincoln called for a half
million more men in 1864—Original negative by
Mathew Brady of Washington

Photograph taken when Lincoln was seeking a General for
all the armies of the Republic in 1864—Negative
by Mathew Brady at Washington

THE SYMPATHY OF LINCOLN FOR THE UNFORTUNATE

 OME men work only with their hands; some with their heads; others with their hearts. A great man works with them all—and of such was Lincoln. He knew that any man who tries to build his life upon any one of these qualities, at the expense of the other, is destined to failure. Lincoln began life with his hands; his first discovery was his heart; and he learned to control them both with his head.

Go back to those days in 1864, and sit with him in his cabinet. The ministers are impatient and stubborn, but he conquers them not with a scourge of discipline but with pointed wit. An officer having some trouble with Sherman, hurries to Lincoln and reports excitedly: "Mr. President, I have a cause of grievance. This morning I went to see Colonel Sherman and he threatened to shoot me!"

"Threatened to shoot you?" exclaims Lincoln in surprise. "Well, if I were you I would not trust him—for I believe he would do it."

Go with Lincoln to the battlefields. Stand beside him as he aims the guns to assure himself of their efficiency, and with his early instinct scores a dozen hits in fourteen shots. Sit with him as he eats at their mess tables and hear him exclaim, "How willingly would I exchange places today with the soldier who sleeps on the ground in the Army of the Potomac."

He knew neither pride of rank nor the glory of war; he touched his hat to the General, but bared his head to the boys in the ranks. The mother's prayer, the father's plea, the babies' cry, the story of an empty sleeve or a crutch, he never failed to hear. Every soldier who carried a musket was his son—all were his children.

"There are already too many weeping widows," he protested when asked to sign execution papers against deserters. "For God's sake, do not ask me to add to the number, for I won't do it!"

A girl is pleading for her brother's life; he has been condemned to die. He is speaking to her: "My poor girl, you have come here with no Governor or Senator or member of Congress to plead your cause; you seem honest and truthful . . . If he has not a friend, I will be his friend!"

A poor widow has lost five sons in battle; he is writing to her: "I pray our Heavenly Father to assuage the anguish of your bereavement and leave only the memory of the loved and lost, and the solemn pride that must be yours to have laid so costly a sacrifice upon the altar of freedom."

Firm and determined—it was the balance of justice.

Photograph of Lincoln taken early in 1864 at the request of Secretary Seward of his cabinet—Original negative by Mathew Brady at Washington— Now in the Collection of Mr. L. C. Handy at Washington

Photograph taken about the time of the Battle of Spottsylvania Court House in 1864—Original negative by Mathew Brady—Deposited in the War Department Collection at Washington

THE WORTH OF A MAN IN LINCOLN'S JUDGMENT

THERE *is a place in the world for every man*—and a man for every place. The secret is in securing the right man for the right place. Lincoln was an experimenter with men. He knew that throughout the annals of mankind, whenever the people are in danger, somewhere, sometime, a man always rises among them to lead their cause.

The Confederacy found such a man to lead their army at the beginning—a man of courage, character, and nobility, a master leader of men. The Union found many men, brave, loyal, conscientious—but it had not yet found the right man for the right place at the right moment. Down in the Mississippi valley, Lincoln's eyes fell upon a little, silent man who was fighting his way through almost insurmountable obstacles; a volunteer, who, without political influence, had offered his services to his country and through his courage was leading his men to victory.

It was early in March, in 1864, that this little, silent man came quietly to Washington. As he passed through the streets, leading his young son by the hand, he wore an old blue uniform; there was a well-worn army hat on his head, and a cigar in his mouth.

A few hours later he entered the White House. Lincoln rose to meet him. His kind, sympathetic face looked down upon the stranger.

"This is Ulysses S. Grant," he exclaimed, and the two men clasped hands. It was a moment that was molding the future of the western world. Here was a man whose life at thirty-nine had been a failure, and, although a graduate of West Point, had never been able to find his right place in the world; who, before the war, was a store clerk at fifty dollars a month.

As Lincoln stood before him, to bestow upon him the highest military honor, which none but Washington among American soldiers had ever borne on the battlefield, ministers of the cabinet gathered about him.

"As the country trusts you," said Lincoln, profoundly, "so under God will it sustain you."

The silent, little man bowed as he took the commission which gave him the destiny of an army. "I feel the full weight of the responsibilities devolving upon me," he said, "and I know that if they are met it will be due to those armies, and above all to the favor of that Providence which loves both nations and men." Declining a public dinner as the guest of the President, he pulled his worn army hat down over his eyes, and left the White House to marshal about him the legions that were now to lead a republic to glorious triumph. The right man was now in the right place.

Photograph of Lincoln about the time that Lincoln met Grant in 1864—
Original negative by Mathew Brady at Washington—Life negative
in Collection of Mr. Frederick H. Meserve of New York

Photograph of Lincoln about the time of Grant's taking command of the
Army in 1864—Original negative by Mathew Brady—Print in
Collection of Mr. Frederick H. Meserve of New York

THE LOYALTY OF LINCOLN TO HIS LIFE WORK

THERE is a halfway point in life where every man hesitates, where he is undecided whether to go ahead or turn back. It is one of the most difficult moments in life, when, not knowing the distance before him, but knowing the distance behind him, he abandons hope with success just around the next turn in the road.

Lincoln never abandoned hope; if he had there would be no United States of America today. "If I go down," he said, "I will go with my colors flying!" But a thousand men with hearts less stout lost hope and appealed to him to turn back, until, in 1864, the whole American people stood at the point of hesitancy. Lincoln had reached the end of the four years' administration to which he had been elected—years of carnage and terror, of death and famine. But the talons of war still clutched the people, tearing their hearts and hopes. Politicians protested that he had been given his opportunity and that he had failed to fulfill his promises. The new Republican party declared that he had wrecked it. His cabinet ministers wavered; one of them offered himself to the people; while Lincoln's friends appealed to him to give up the struggle.

"I have pledged myself," he replied, "to save the Union!"

The radicals in the Republican party met in convention and nominated one of Lincoln's generals in the army for President. The Democrats were pledged to nominate another of Lincoln's generals to succeed him; both appealed to the people with the declaration that "the war is a failure," and promised to end the terrible slaughter.

Lincoln answered them with but one appeal: "I believe that the people will give me a chance to finish the work that I have begun." The sense of fair play always surges through the masses. "Give Lincoln a chance," came back the response from the plain people. The sentiment passed through the country.

When Lincoln heard of his re-nomination as the standard bearer of the National Union League, he felt that the American people were still with him, although he knew that the political powers would conspire to overwhelm and defeat their purpose.

"I do not allow myself to suppose," he said, "that they have concluded that I am either the greatest or best man in America, but rather they have concluded that it is not best to swap horses while crossing a stream." The homely phrase caught the spirit of the American people, and Lincoln again stood before them as their candidate for President.

LINCOLN ABOUT THE TIME OF HIS SECOND NOMINATION FOR THE
PRESIDENCY OF THE UNITED STATES

Photograph taken in 1864 when the political leaders were declaring that Lincoln could not
be re-elected and the American people were demanding his leadership—
Original negative by Walker in Washington

Print from the Collection of Mr. Osborn H. Oldroyd at the Lincoln Museum at Washington

Photograph of Lincoln at the time of his second nomination for the
Presidency, in 1864—Original negative by Mathew Brady—From
Collection of Americana of Frederick H. Meserve

Photograph of Lincoln with his son Thomas (Tad) in 1864
Original negative by Mathew Brady at Washington

LINCOLN WITH HIS SON, THOMAS, (TAD) IN THE WHITE HOUSE

Photograph taken with Lincoln in his characteristic attitude at home
with his eleven years-old son by his side—His son William
Wallace had died at the White House two years before

Original negative by Mathew Brady in Collection of Mr. L. C. Handy at Washington

THE INSIGHT OF LINCOLN INTO HUMAN NATURE

A WORD of wisdom is worth more than volumes of argument. The shaft of reason has frequently won victories while armies are meeting defeat. The summer of 1864 was long and disappointing. The success of the great armies swung back and forth with almost endless precision. Now the war was to end; now the conflict raged fiercer than ever; now again the Confederacy seemed shattered; only to rise once more in brave defiance.

"I propose to fight it out on this line if it takes all summer," came the message from the silent, little general on the battle-line.

Political leaders insisted that Lincoln could never be re-elected. Business interests grew more and more doubtful. The Stars and Bars swept so close to the national capital that Lincoln looked into the firing line. The North was in panic. Preparations were made for abandoning Washington. A steamer was in readiness to take the President and his cabinet to safety. The wounded and the sick poured into the city.

"We must have more men!" said Lincoln. His demand for five hundred thousand more fighting men from the states staggered the politicians.

"Lincoln must withdraw his candidacy," demanded the political leaders. "Patriotism demands his retirement. He has proved that he cannot meet the necessities of the emergency."

"Don't swap horses while crossing a stream," was the only reply that came from the man in the White House.

Suddenly the nation was aroused by the message from the battlefield: "Atlanta is ours and fairly won! Sherman is marching to the sea! The Northern forces are sweeping down the valley of the Shenandoah!"

Election day came on the eighth of November. Lincoln spent the day at his desk in the war office, expressing more interest in the messages from the battlefield than the political conflict. About midnight the wire ticked: "Lincoln has carried every state in the Union except three. He has been re-elected President by a majority of nearly a half million votes!"

As he walked in the darkness to the White House, he found a party of serenaders under the window of his chamber. It was about two o'clock in the morning. "Friends," he exclaimed, "if I know my heart, my gratitude is free from any intent of personal triumph. I do not impugn the motive of anyone who opposed me. It is no pleasure to me to triumph over anyone, but I give thanks to the Almighty for this evidence of the people's resolution to stand by free government and the rights of humanity."

Photograph of Lincoln about the time of his second election as
President in 1864—Original negative by Walker, photographer
for the Treasury Department at Washington—Print from
Collection of Mr. Frederick H. Meserve of New York

Photograph of Lincoln, age 56 years, shortly before his second
inauguration in 1865—Original negative by Alexander
Gardner at Washington—Print from the Collection
of Mr. Frederick H. Meserve of New York

THE HEART OF LINCOLN THAT KNEW NO MALICE

THERE are a few men who can forgive their enemies but it takes a great man to forget them. Lincoln forgot all animosity when he forgave. He found that 2,216,067 Americans had pledged their loyalty to him at polls, while 1,808,725 had registered their ballots against him under the leadership of his former friend, General McClellan. The cabinet minister, who in envy had tried to take the presidency from him, and had resigned in indignation, was honored by Lincoln with the highest tribute that the President can confer—Chief Justice of the United States Supreme Court. He lived by the Golden Rule. "If any man ceases to attack me, I never remember the past against him," he said. "We must not be animated by any motive for revenge, or any purpose to punish for punishment's sake."

It was now the fourth of March, in 1865—the day of inauguration. A light rain was falling in the chill and gloom. A carriage stopped at the White House door, and Lincoln came down the steps and entered it, alone.

It was about two o'clock in the afternoon. A curious crowd had gathered around the national capitol; negroes, who were but yesterday slaves, and citizens jostled each other in the crowd to catch a glimpse of "Father Abraham." Four years had wrought great changes in the scene. Statesmen who had then gathered here, were now dead; while others were now battling on the firing line; and still others had renounced the Republic.

As Lincoln appeared on the steps a rousing cheer greeted him. His stooping shoulders, and sunken eyes, told the tragic story. As he looked out over the applauding throng, a stream of sick and wounded heroes were coming in endless procession from the fields of battle.

"Fellow countrymen." The words brought a hush to the gathering. The tall, solemn figure spoke in inspiration. "Let us judge not that we be not judged," he said. "Fondly do we hope, fervently do we pray that this scourge of war may speedily pass away." The great audience listened. The closing words rested upon them like a benediction: "With malice toward none, with charity for all, with firmness in the right, as God gives us to see the light, let us stand on to finish the work we are in; to bind up the nation's wounds; to care for him who shall have won the battle and for his widow, and his orphan; and do all which may achieve and cherish a just and lasting peace among races and with all nations." As he stood before the cheering throng, the sun, which had been veiled by rain throughout the day, burst through the clouds in splendor.

Photograph of Lincoln in the closing days of the American
Crisis in 1865—Original negative by Alexander Gardner
at Washington—Print from the Collection of Mr. L.
C. Handy in Washington, District of Columbia

Photograph of Lincoln at his second inauguration in 1865,
age 56 years—Original negative by H. F. Warren, Waltham,
Massachusetts—Print in the Collection of Mr. Osborn H.
Oldroyd at the Lincoln Museum in Washington

THE FATHERHOOD OF LINCOLN AMONG THE LOWLY

*T*HE *fortunes of war are much like the fortunes of men.* While Lincoln was winning his battles over the people, his silent, little general was carrying the armies to victory. With irresistible power he was driving back the Confederacy and marching on to their seat of government. A messenger hurried to the White House with a dispatch. Lincoln read it and then sat pondering over its contents.

"I must go to the front," he said. "They may need me." The next night a boat steamed up the James River. There, lying on a berth, four inches shorter than his body, stretched a long, gaunt figure. The roar of the battle rolled along the shore.

"Richmond has fallen! The Confederacy is destroyed! The capital is burning!" The tidings aroused the continent; leaped the oceans, and resounded around the world. The North was wild with joy. The South was bowed with grief. Brave hearts shouted and wept; cheered and sighed. The noble city burst into flames. With the rumble of the drums, and colors flying, the hosts of the Republic marched into the fallen capital.

It was the month of April, in 1865. The sun rose clear on the morning of the fourth. At twelve o'clock the barge reached the river bank. As it came alongside, the tall, gaunt man stepped ashore. An old negro with snow white hair was standing on the bank. He was bent and worn.

"Bless de Lord," he shouted, "dere is de great Messiah! I knowed him as soon as I seed him. He's been in my mind fo' long yeahs, an' he's cum at las' to free his chilun from deir bondage—Glory Hallelujah!"

And, falling on his knees, the old slave kissed the feet of Lincoln. The negroes crowded about him and threw themselves on the ground. Lincoln looked at the poor creatures before him. "Don't kneel to me," he said quietly. "That is not right. You must kneel to God only, and thank Him for the liberty you will hereafter enjoy."

"Father Abraham is here!" The streets were instantly alive with the colored race. They seemed to spring from the earth, tumbling, shouting, weeping, praying, singing. There stood the Emancipator among the people he had redeemed from bondage.

"My poor friends," he said, "you are free—free as air. You can cast off the name of slave and trample upon it; it will come to you no more. Liberty is your birthright. God gave it to you as he gave it to others . . . Let the world see that you merit it, and are able to maintain it by your good works . . . There, now let me pass on."

PRESIDENT LINCOLN ABOUT THE TIME OF THE FALL OF RICHMOND IN 1865

Photograph taken a few days before Lincoln went to the capital of the Confederacy
to look upon the ruins of the historic city—Original negative by Mathew Brady

Deposited in the Original Brady Collection at Springfield, Massachusetts
Copyright, 1909, by Mr. Edward Bailey Eaton

THE MAGNANIMITY OF THE SPIRIT OF LINCOLN

*L*IFE'S *great question is not alone how did you bear yourself in defeat,* but how did you bear yourself in victory. As Lincoln walked through the streets of the destroyed capital of the Confederacy, his eyes looked upon ruin and devastation; starvation and pillage. The flames were still smoldering in the noble capital.

Before him stood the White House of the Confederacy, from which, only thirty-six hours before, the statesmen of the "Lost Cause" had fled for safety. Ascending the steps, he entered the stately mansion. There lay a great desk, with a huge chair, deserted.

"It must have been President Davis' chair," he said, as he sank into it wearily, relaxing himself against its comfortable back and resting his hands on its arms. The lines upon his forehead deepened. "Judge not," he said, thoughtfully, "that ye be not judged!"

The boat bearing Lincoln sailed up the Potomac, to take him back to the capital of the Republic at Washington. His eyes fell upon the white dome. An expression of dread came to the face of Mrs. Lincoln, who was now with him. "That city," she whispered, in apprehension, "is full of our enemies!" Lincoln turned, and with perplexed expression, he exclaimed, "Enemies!—we must never speak that word again!"

The evening was falling. Mount Vernon loomed in the distance. Lincoln looked out into the gathering twilight. "Springfield!" he said, in reverie. "How happy, four years hence to return there in peace and tranquility!"

The Nation's capital was waiting in expectancy. The air was rent with exploding rockets. Crowds gathered in front of the White House and cheered. The throngs outside called for "Lincoln! Lincoln!"

"Fellow Citizens," he said, "We meet this evening not in sorrow but in gladness of heart . . . In the happiness of all this, however, Him from Whom all blessings flow must not be forgotten. I call for a National Thanksgiving which is being prepared and will be duly promulgated."

A great cheer arose from the serenaders. The martial notes of the "Star Spangled Banner" passed through the crowd. Lincoln stood with his head bared. As the refrain ceased, he raised his hand and called: "Give us Dixie! We have a right to that tune now!" As he turned and entered the White House, the strains of the hymn of the South-land fell upon his ears and echoed through his heart. "This," he said, "is one of the happiest moments of my life."

LINCOLN AT THE END OF THE CIVIL WAR AND THE SURRENDER AT APPOMATTOX

Photograph taken in Washington in 1865 shortly before the Hosts of the South and the
Legions of the North clasped hands in Peace—Original negative by Mathew
Brady now considered the greatest portrait of Lincoln ever taken

Deposited in the Original Brady Collection at Springfield, Massachusetts
Copyright, 1908, by Mr. Edward Bailey Eaton

THE VICTORY OF LINCOLN—A REUNITED PEOPLE

*P*EACE *hath its victories no less than war.* Through all the four years of magnificent courage there is not a moment more inspiring than that April day when the hosts of the South stood before the legions of the North to pledge themselves to peace and brotherhood. In an heroic stand, the warriors of the Confederacy had made their last gallant charge under the Stars and Bars. Now they stood before the victorious warriors of the Republic, welcoming peace with the same brave hearts with which they faced battle.

The two greatest generals that the world has ever known stood face to face—Grant and Lee. Behind them were the armies in the mightiest struggle that has ever been recorded in human annals. There stood the silent, little general, the conqueror, in his uniform of blue; his figure, of five feet eight inches, slightly bent; there was no sword in his hand; only his shoulder straps to designate him from the rank of a private soldier. There stood the gallant leader of the Confederacy in his uniform of gray; his silver hair crowning his erect figure of six feet in height; at his side he carried a long sword, the hilt studded with jewels.

The war was over. The camp fires were left to smolder into ashes; the flags were tenderly furled; and two great armies sheathed their swords. Along the roads moved regiments of men, no longer foes, but citizens of a common country. The rattle of the artillery; the rumbling wheels of the ammunition trains; all in the pageant of peace—echoed through the streets.

Lincoln stood and gazed long upon them. The long night of bloodshed had ended. The day of peace and love had dawned. He looked upon a portrait of the conquered commander of the Confederacy.

"It is a good face," he said. "It is the face of a noble, brave man. I am glad that the war is over at last. We soon will live with the brave men who have been fighting against us. I trust that the era of good feeling has returned and that henceforth we will live in peace."

And, turning to his family, his heart trying to lift the veil of tragedy that had so long enshrouded it, he said: "It is nearly over; now we shall be happy." Throughout the hills and dales resounded the shouts of rejoicing. Mothers clasped their long lost sons to their hearts; and children climbed into the arms of their fathers who had come home at last.

The war was over! The miracle of the reunited people had been performed. And above it all loomed the tall, strong figure of one man— Abraham Lincoln.

LAST PORTRAIT OF LINCOLN EVER TAKEN

Photograph taken a few days before the end of Lincoln's life in April, 1865,
when the War was over and the American People were re-united
into an inseparable brotherhood—Original negative
by Alexander Gardner at Washington

Collection of Mr. M. P. Rice of Washington—Copyright, 1891

THE VEIL OF SORROW OVER AN EXULTANT NATION

NO man knows what the morrow may bring forth. We live today, but what of the morning? The morning of the fourteenth of April, in 1865, was bright and warm. The balm of spring bathed the hills. The Judas and the dog-wood bent in the the breeze; the perfume of the lilacs floated through the morning air.

It was Good Friday, the nation's day of prayer and thanksgiving. Lincoln rose early. A great weight seemed to have lifted. Today he was to clasp the hand of Grant, the silent, little general who had led his armies to triumph. Today the flag of the republic, which had been lowered from Fort Sumter four years ago, was to be unfurled over the ruins. Today his oldest son was to return from the war with a captain's commission.

As Lincoln took his seat at the head of the cabinet table, his grave, sad eyes smiled; the haggard lines in his face seemed to disappear. He greeted his ministers with words of affection, and, as he dropped his arm upon the shoulders of one of his statesmen, he drew him close to him in hearty embrace in their rejoicing over the end of the mighty struggle.

"The war is over," he said. "Enough lives have been sacrificed. We must extinguish all resentment if we expect harmony and Union."

He grasped the hands of his cabinet ministers, and, entreating them to be considerate of the vanquished foes, he left them and was soon driving with his wife along the country roads on this beautiful spring day.

As the carriage rumbled along the blossom-laden lanes, he turned to her and said: "Mary, we have had a hard time of it since we came to Washington, but the war is over, and with God's permission we may hope for four years of happiness and peace, and then we will go back to Illinois and pass the rest of our lives in quiet."

He spoke of the old home in Springfield, and the recollections of his early days came crowding back to him. He spoke of their early struggles together and of their future. "We have laid by some money," he said "and during this term we will try to save up more. Then we will go home."

The night fell. Throughout the nation, in a hundred thousand homes, loved ones were gathering in reunion and thanksgiving. Now and then there was a cheer, or the beat of a drum at the head of the soldiers marching home. Suddenly, a great tumult arose in the streets. Newsboys ran excitedly over the pavements. Great throngs gathered at the bulletins.

"Lincoln has been assassinated! The President has been shot!"

The crowds in the streets seemed stunned.

The Portrait Life of Lincoln

PART III

A Revelation of the Last Scenes in the
Closing Hours of Lincoln
from Actual Photographs Taken at the Time

THE LAST LINGERING MOMENTS OF A NOBLE LIFE

THIS *is life's greatest moment*—it comes to us all. It matters not how great or how humble we may be, we are all one at the end; the millions that have gone before, the millions that are to come.

As Lincoln, on that tragic night, on the fourteenth of April, entered the box at the theater, in honor of the dawning peace, the orchestral strains of "Hail to the Chief" greeted him. The great audience rose to its feet and cheered. Lincoln bowed. It was a gala night. The spirit of joyousness filled every heart. The audience roared with laughter over the farcical lines of the mimic world on the stage.

Suddenly, a shot rang through the theater. There was the scream of a woman. The figure of a man, an actor, sprang from the Presidential box, his eyes gleaming with passion. A smoking pistol fell from his hand as he clutched at a dagger. His spur caught in an American flag, and he fell upon the stage with the ensign wound about him. Raising his knife in the air, his words echoed above the tumult: "Sic semper tyrannis!"

The great audience was in frenzy; aisles and seats and galleries were filled with shouting, weeping, panic-stricken men and women; the crowd became uncontrollable. "My God, the President is shot!" sobbed strong men, while women fainted.

The body of Lincoln was lifted from his chair; his head drooped; blood was flowing from a wound. Over him, moaned his wife, pleading for him to speak. Gently they bore him from the theater. As they passed to the street, and carried him to the nearest house, their steps were marked by his ebbing blood. Behind them walked Mrs. Lincoln, weeping.

Great throngs crowded about the humble dwelling. Anxiously they waited for a message. The curtains were drawn at the windows. All night long the crowds lingered; now they were silent under the burden of grief; now bitterness rankled within them as its meaning flooded upon them.

At the White House, not far distant, all was still. Suddenly the east door of the basement was thrown open. "Oh Tom! Tom!" cried a little voice. "They have killed papa dead! They have killed papa dead!" and he burst into sobs. It was little Tad. He threw himself into the arms of an old family servant.

"Now, now, boy," said the faithful friend, caressing him, "don't cry any more; let's go to bed." They turned down the cover and lay down together. The old servant put his arm around the grief-stricken lad; the sobs died away, and Tad fell into sound sleep.

Photograph taken at Ford's Theater in Washington, after the assassination on the night of April 14, 1865—Original negatives by Alexander Gardner—Now deposited in the Original Brady Collection of seven thousand negatives at Springfield, Massachusetts

Photograph of President Lincoln's box in Ford's Theater as it appeared on night of the tragedy

Photograph of the chair in which President Lincoln was sitting when he was shot by John Wilkes Booth

THE MAGNIFICENCE OF LIFE'S LAST TRIUMPH

AND after all—what does it mean for a man to live well? Come to that little chamber in the dingy brick building across the way. The stairs are dark and narrow. Walk softly through the long, dim hall. There is a door; knock gently; someone is opening it; there are tears in his eyes.

Step into the room—the simple bedchamber of a soldier. The flickering light of a gas-jet falls upon the pallid face of a man that you love. How pale and sad it is! The long, gaunt figure that you have known so long, how motionless it lies!

A moan comes from a grief-pent heart; the arms are lifted; now they fall; there is a long sigh. A smile comes to the face and rests upon it; how restful it is, like the benediction of peace. How long the night seems! How still it is: only the footfalls of the loved ones—and a sob!

The April rain is falling. Daylight sends its first gray rays through the window. The notes of the robin float on the morning breeze. Statesmen are gathering about the bed; army generals and senators stand with bowed heads. How white the face looks in the morning light. The pale cheeks flush; the lips seem to part; a magnificent light leaps from the deep, sunken eyes. A physician is leaning over the figure; his ear is close to the heart. The clock is ticking. He speaks: "The President is dead!"

A clergyman kneels by the bedside. A cabinet minister leans over the ashen face and gazes for a moment into it—how happy it looks! Then, tenderly stroking the lids with his hands, he closes the kind eyes in their last, long sleep, and, drawing a sheet over the slumbering man, his voice speaks low and deep: "Now he belongs to the ages!"

The hands of the clock on the mantel point at twenty-two minutes after seven. It is Saturday morning. Tomorrow will be Easter Sunday. The statesmen bow, and pass from the room. A woman falls upon the lifeless form; oh, how she sobs; her loving heart is breaking! Close the door gently; leave them alone in life's greatest moment—a moment that you and I must soon meet—life's last triumph!

Was there ever a scene more magnificent? Was there ever a greater victory? Was there ever a man whose tribute from the world was more beautiful? Look at the thousands and the hundreds of thousands passing before his bier—looking into the face that they loved—men, women, and children, weeping; all races and sects knit together into one kinship—his beloved children.

House in which President Lincoln Died on Saturday Morning April 15, 1865

Photograph taken of the building opposite Ford's Theater in which Lincoln
spent his last hours—The house is now the famous Lincoln Museum
established by Mr. Osborn H. Oldroyd at Washington, D. C.
Print in possession of Mr. L. C. Handy of Washington

THE INFAMY OF A DEED THAT ROBBED A NATION

AND *after all—what does it mean for a man to live ill?* The world turned in wrath against the murderers of the man who had loved humanity. Bitterness raged in their hearts against the assassins. Their names, which are hardly fit to speak, except as they stand as ignominious warning to mankind, aroused only the hatred of their fellow-men, and, like all who break the laws of God and man, are passing down through the generations to be loathed.

The assassin, who, craving for notoriety, had fired the fatal shot in the theater, fled from the stage in the excitement. His leg broken by the fall from the balcony, he escaped on a horse that was waiting for him in the streets, all the fast closing hours of his life to be haunted as a creature too low to be allowed to exist even in the blood of his own crime.

Pitiful figure that he was, cursed by his own morbid longings, and believing that the world might look upon and glorify him for his daring, he found himself riding into the mouth of hell. Slowly, but surely, the grip of the law tightened about him. Driven to desperation, he took his last refuge in a barn on a Virginia farm, only to see his last friend betray him.

As the flames leaped from his place of refuge, he rose from his crouching position and stood upright, leaning upon a crutch, and holding a carbine. His eyes glared with the light of fever; his face was haggard from eleven days of the most fearful torture that a man can endure. There was a flash from a cavalry rifle. The crutch fell at his side. A long groan came from his lips; his face writhed in agony—he had paid the penalty.

Look upon him with all the pity that is within your heart—poor, unfortunate, deluded man. In his moment of ambition he forgot the ruling hand of Justice that no man ever was or ever will be able to overpower. He forgot that while, for a time, we may withstand it, there is within every man's heart a law that he never can escape—the law of conscience.

As they carried his body away, to give it a secret resting place that no man will ever know, a diary fell from his pocket. In it was scribbled the last words of an agonized heart: "Hunted like a dog through the swamps . . . I am here in despair . . . I am abandoned with the curse of Cain upon me."

And turn now to the prison yard. There on the gallows hang the bodies of those, who, in their blindness, were led into this plot. There in the prison cell sit those who listened to false ambition—now rejected and despised by their fellow-men. Look upon them all with pity!

Photograph of John Wilkes Booth, the actor, who shot Lincoln
at Ford's Theater, Friday night, April 14, 1865

Photograph of Sergeant Boston Corbett, 16th New York Cavalry,
who fired the shot that killed the fugitive Booth in a
barn in Virginia at 3:15 a.m., April 26, 1865

Negatives in the Original Brady-Gardner Collection
at Springfield, Massachusetts

Mrs. Mary E. Surratt, an unfortunate widow and mother, whose home unwittingly became the center of the conspiracy

George Atzerodt, a carriage painter, who, it was charged, was delegated to assassinate Vice-President Johnson

Davey Herold, the boy who aided Booth to escape, and left his mother and seven sisters heartbroken

Lewis Payne (Powell), a Florida boy, in double irons—He attempted to assassinate Seward in his home

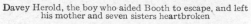

HANGED AS CONSPIRATORS IN ASSASSINATION OF LINCOLN

Original Secret Service Negatives in the Brady-Gardner Collection at Springfield, Massachusetts

Michael O'Laughlin, sentenced for life and died during imprisonment; his remains were sent to his mother

Sam Arnold, clerk in sutler's store, sentenced for life but pardoned after serving four years

Edward Spangler, scene shifter, sentenced to six years; pardoned in four years and died 18 months later

Dr. Samuel A. Mudd, physician, who, for harboring Booth was sentenced for life; pardoned after four years

IMPRISONED AS ACCESSORIES IN ASSASSINATION OF LINCOLN

Original Secret Service Negatives in the Brady-Gardner Collection at Springfield, Massachusetts

PRISON WHERE THE CONSPIRATORS WERE CONFINED—Photograph taken at the old penitentiary building on the Arsenal grounds at Washington where the accused were imprisoned in cells and heavily chained and manacled—Original negative in the Brady-Gardner Collection deposited in Springfield, Massachusetts

MILITARY COURT THAT TRIED THE LINCOLN CONSPIRATORS—Photograph taken when the commission began to take testimony on May 12, 1865—Lieutenant General Grant, whose life was also in the conspiracy, was the first witness—Print in the Collection of Americana of Mr. Frederick H. Meserve of New York

GALLOWS IN THE PRISON YARD WHERE THE CONSPIRATORS WERE HANGED—
Photograph taken on the afternoon of July 7, 1865 when the ropes were being noosed
about the conspirators—Original negative by Alexander Gardner, government
photographer, now in Brady-Gardner Collection in Springfield, Massachusetts

EXECUTION OF THE CONVICTED PRISONERS IN THE LINCOLN ASSASSINATION—
This remarkable negative is a silent witness of the end of one of the world's
greatest tragedies—Taken by Alexander Gardner while those who paid
penalty were hanging on gallows—Negative in Springfield, Massachusetts

THE GLORY OF A MAN WHO LOVES HIS FELLOW-MEN

WHAT, then, do we learn from the life of such a man as Abraham Lincoln? It is the simplest, plainest truth in all history—the greatest man in the world is the man who loves his fellow-men. Kings come and go; nations rise and fall; military glory and political eminence flare for their moment and then die away. Men may erect great monuments to their memory; genius may leave its marvels behind it; masters may build their powerful institutions,—but there is only one living force that pulsates through the ages and that is the heart of man himself.

Let your eyes rest upon Lincoln, not with the din of battle in your ears, not with the shout of victory nor the pangs of defeat in your heart, but as a man who knew no malice, who knew no envy, who knew no glory,—but who knew only that he loved his fellow-men and that he was one of the most humble among them.

The funeral train moves slowly from the nation's capital; watch-fires blaze in the darkness as it passes; bells are tolling. Was there ever a procession like this—nearly two thousand miles of a people's tribute! Twenty-five million fellow-men bowing their heads in prayer.

Now he is home at last—home again in Springfield, where he longed to rest after his work was done. It is May-day the fourth. Tenderly, they are bearing him to the foot of the wooded knoll; they are laying him in the shade of the oaks.

Hark! Can you hear the melody? From every mountain and valley; from every state and clime—the solemn strains of the dirge are swelling.

The sun drops over the hills. Twilight bathes the blossoming foliage and gathers its darkening shadows about the tomb. The world has lost a simple, honest man—and immortality has gained one. From every nation and from every people, from farm and bench and throne of monarchs, come tributes of his greatness; for days and months they came; for years and for decades they have been coming, and ever will as long as memory shall last and men shall love an honest heart.

This is the true Lincoln—the Lincoln that you should know; the Lincoln the generations will know when they have forgotten that blinding war of brother against brother, and come to grasp the hand of this great, strong, homely man among men. This is the Lincoln that the world will love—the common heritage of all races and times—the man with a heart big enough to hold the whole world.

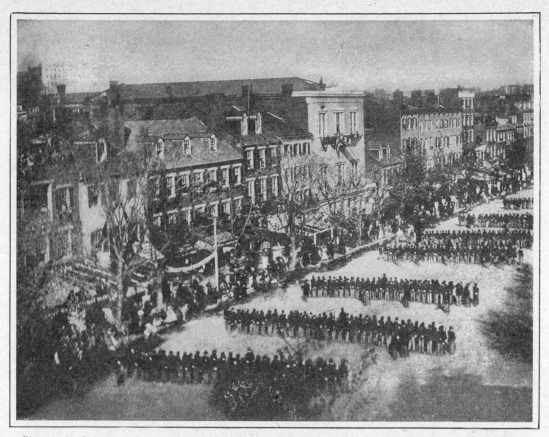

Photograph of the funeral procession of Lincoln passing through the streets of Washington at the beginning of the sixteen hundred mile journey of triumph to his old home at Springfield, Illinois, on April 21, 1865—Negative by Gardner

Bier on which President Lincoln rested in state while men, women, and children wept over their lost leader on his funeral day on April 19, 1865, when twenty-five million people throughout the country bowed their heads in tribute—Original negatives by Alexander Gardner now deposited in the Brady-Gardner Collection at Springfield, Massachusetts

Photograph of Funeral Catafalque of Lincoln passing through Philadelphia

Photograph while Lincoln's body lay in state before great throngs at City Hall in New York

Photograph of the funeral car bearing the dead Lincoln back to Springfield, Illinois
Prints from the Collection of Mr. Frederick H. Meserve of New York

Lincoln is "home at last"—Photograph as they are laying Lincoln in his tomb in beautiful Oak Ridge Cemetery in Springfield, Illinois, on May 4, 1865

Tomb of Lincoln where he was left with a soldier's guard by a mourning nation—Prints from the Collection of Mr. Frederick H. Meserve of New York

A Nation's Tribute to Lincoln

Magnificent Memorial at Lincoln's burial-place in his old home city
of Springfield, Illinois—Massive marble shaft rising above
the catacomb and memorial hall proclaims the simple
greatness of the man whom the whole world loves

Photograph taken shortly after its erection in 1874, showing the original tomb
at the foot of the hill where Lincoln lay for nine years

Print in the Collection of Americana owned by Mr. Frederick H. Meserve of New York

The Portrait Life of Lincoln

PART IV

The Nine Great Speeches that Mark the
Rise of Abraham Lincoln
as an Orator and Leader of the People

FIRST PUBLIC SPEECH OF ABRAHAM LINCOLN

Delivered at twenty-three years of age when "Honest Abe" the country store
clerk at New Salem, Illinois, became a candidate for the Legislature, in 1832

FELLOW-CITIZENS: I presume you all know who I am. I am
humble Abraham Lincoln. I have been solicited by many friends to become
a candidate for the Legislature. My politics are short and sweet, like the
old woman's dance. I am in favor of a national bank. I am in favor of the
internal improvement system, and a high protective tariff. These are my
sentiments and political principles. If elected, I shall be thankful; if not,
it will be all the same.

LINCOLN left his own written record of his character and intellect
in his speeches. They are the living witnesses that remain long
after human lips are silent. In them is woven the true life-story
of the man.

Oratory has always been the forerunner of the world's civilization. It is the resounding voice of the future. In modern times, oratory has
not aroused the people as it did of old, owing to the democracy of the public
press which now speaks to the whole world while the human voice can
reach but the few who are within its hearing. The art of oratory will,
nevertheless, always remain one of the greatest gifts of genius.

Lincoln lived in a day when oratory was the road to greatness. His first
public speech, in its homely candor, is much like the first experiences of most
men when they find themselves before their first audience. He was the backwoods youth, but twenty-three years of age, when he delivered this first
speech; he neither knew nor was known by the world. In it, however, is the
beginning of his journey. It epitomizes the political principles that were the
foundation of his strength and character throughout his life.

In these pages are recorded the nine great speeches that mark the rise of
Lincoln as the leader of his people. He occupied the platform on nearly all
public occasions and spoke on all the varied subjects from temperance to
invention. It was not until he met Douglas in debate that his speeches were
very widely known. He was fifty-one years of age when he made his first
appearance in the East as an orator, and delivered his first national speech
at the Cooper Union mass meeting in New York. From this time he became
one of the great American orators and his speeches had a deeper effect upon
the trend of events than those of any other man of the generation. His
inaugural addresses inspired the nation, while his speech at Gettysburg has
taken its place as one of the world's greatest orations.

Lincoln was not the turgid rhetorician of the old-school of statesmanship,
but a simple, logical reasoner. His words did not inflame the imagination;
they carried conviction. While it is estimated that Lincoln delivered nearly
a hundred speeches many of them were extemporaneous and cannot be recorded.
Others were not reported at the time and there are various versions of them.
The nine speeches given here are the result of long research through authoritative sources. They represent the turning points in Lincoln's life and accu-
rately establish the nine progressive steps through which he rose from a back-
woodsman to the highest political honor in the world.

FIRST GREAT PATRIOTIC SPEECH OF LINCOLN

Delivered at twenty-eight years of age, while a member of the Legislature of
Illinois, before the Young Men's Lyceum, at Springfield, on January 27, 1837

IN the great journal of things happening under the sun, we, the American people, find our account running the date of the nineteenth century of the Christian era. We find ourselves in the peaceful possession of the fairest portion of the earth as regards extent of territory, fertility of soil, and salubrity of climate. We find ourselves under the government of a system of political institutions conducing more essentially to the ends of the civil and religious liberty than any of which the history of former times tells us. We, when mounting the stage of existence, found ourselves the legal inheritors of these fundamental blessings. We toiled not in the acquirement or establishment of them; they are a legacy bequeathed to us by once a hardy, brave, and patriotic, but now lamented and departed, race of our ancestors. Theirs was the task (and nobly they performed it) to possess themselves, and through themselves us, of this goodly land, and to uprear upon its hills and its valleys a political edifice of liberty and equal rights; 'tis ours only to transmit these— the former unprofaned by the foot of an invader, the latter undecayed by the lapse of time and untorn by usurpation—to the latest generation that fate shall permit the world to know. This task of gratitude to our fathers, justice to ourselves, duty to posterity, and love for our species in general, all imperatively require us faithfully to perform.

How then shall we perform it? At what point shall we expect the approach of danger? By what means shall we fortify against it? Shall we expect some transatlantic military giant to step the ocean and crush us at a blow? Never! All the armies of Europe, Asia, and Africa combined, with all the treasure of the earth (our own excepted) in their military chest, with a Bonaparte for a commander, could not by force take a drink from the Ohio or make a track on the Blue Ridge in a trial of a thousand years.

At what point is the approach of danger to be expected? I answer, if it ever reach us, it must spring up amongst us; it cannot come from abroad. If destruction be our lot, we must ourselves be its author and finisher. As a nation of free men, we must live through all time, or die by suicide.

I hope I am not over wary; but if I am not there is even now something of ill omen amongst us. I mean the increasing disregard for law which pervades the country—the growing disposition to substitute the wild and furious passions in lieu of the sober judgment of courts, and the worse than savage mobs for the executive ministers of justice. This disposition is awfully fearful in any community; and that it now exists in ours, though grating to our feelings to admit, it would be a violation of truth and an insult to our intelligence to deny. Accounts of outrages committed by mobs form the every-day news of the times. They have pervaded the country from New England to Louisiana; they are neither peculiar to the eternal snows of the former nor the burning suns of the latter; they are not the creature of climate, neither are they confined to the slave-holding or the non-slave-holding States. Alike they spring up among the pleasure-hunting masters of Southern slaves, and the order-loving citizens of the land of steady habits. Whatever then their cause may be, it is common to the whole country.

It would be tedious as well as useless to recount the horrors of all of them.

Mob Law Is the Greatest Danger of the Nation

Those happening in the State of Mississippi and at St. Louis are perhaps the most dangerous in example, and the most revolting to humanity. In the Mississippi case, they first commenced by hanging the regular gamblers—a set of men certainly not following for a livelihood a very useful or honest occupation, but one which, so far from being forbidden by the laws was actually licensed by an act of the legislature passed but a single year before. Next, negroes suspected of conspiring to raise an insurrection were caught up and hanged in all parts of the State; then, white men supposed to be leagued with the negroes; and finally, strangers from neighboring States, going thither on business, were in many instances subjected to the same fate. Thus went on this process of hanging, from gamblers to negroes, from negroes to white citizens, and from these to strangers, until dead men were seen literally dangling from boughs of trees upon every roadside, and in numbers almost sufficient to rival the native Spanish moss of the country as a drapery to the forest.

Turn then to that horror-striking scene at St. Louis. A single victim was only sacrificed there. This story is very short, and is perhaps the most highly tragic of anything of its length that has ever been witnessed in real life. A mulatto man by the name of McIntosh was seized in the street, dragged to the suburbs of the city, chained to a tree, and actually burned to death; and all within a single hour from the time when he had been a free man attending to his own business and at peace with the world.

Such are the effects of mob law, and such are the scenes becoming more and more frequent in this land so lately famed for love of law and order, and the stories of which have even now grown too familiar to attract anything more than an idle remark.

But you are perhaps ready to ask, "What has this to do with the perpetuation of our political institutions?" I answer, "It has much to do with it." Its direct consequences are, comparatively speaking, but a small evil, and much of its danger consists in the proneness of our minds to regard its direct as its only consequences. Abstractly considered, the hanging of the gamblers at Vicksburg was of but little consequence. They constitute a portion of population that is worse than useless in any community; and their death, if no pernicious example is set by it, is never a matter of reasonable regret by anyone. If they were annually swept from the stage of existence by the plague or smallpox, honest men would perhaps be much profited by the operation. Similar, too is the correct reasoning in regard to the burning of the negro at St. Louis. He had forfeited his life by the perpetration of an outrageous murder upon one of the most worthy and respectable citizens of the city, and had he not died as he did, he must have died by the sentence of the law a short time afterward. As to him alone, it was as well the way it was as it could otherwise have been. But the example in either case was fearful. When men take it into their heads to-day to hang gamblers or burn murderers, they should recollect that in the confusion usually attending such transactions, they will be as likely to hang or burn someone who is neither a gambler nor a murderer as one who is, and that, acting upon the example they set, the mob of to-morrow may, and probably will, hang or burn some of them by the same mistake. And not only so; the innocent, those who have ever set their faces against violations of law in every shape, alike with the guilty, fall victims to the ravages of mob law; and thus it goes on, step by step, 'til all the walls erected for the defense of the persons and property of individuals are trodden down and disregarded. But all this, even, is not the full extent of the evil. By such examples, by instances of the perpetrators of such acts going unpunished, the lawless in spirit are encouraged to become lawless in practice; and having been used to no restraint but dread of punishment, they thus become absolutely unrestrained. Having ever regarded government as their deadliest bane, they make a jubilee of the suspension of its operations, and pray for nothing so much as its total annihilation. While, on the other hand, good men, men who love tranquillity, who desire to abide by the laws and enjoy their benefits, who would gladly spill their blood in the defense of their country, seeing their property destroyed, their families insulted, and their lives endangered, their persons injured, and seeing nothing in prospect that forebodes a change for the better, become tired of and disgusted with a government that offers them no protection, and are not much averse to a change in which they imagine they have nothing to lose. Thus, then, by the operation of this mobocratic spirit which all must admit is now abroad in the land, the strongest bulwark of governments, and particularly of those constituted like ours, may effectually be broken down and destroyed—I mean the attachment of the people. Whenever this effect shall be produced among us; whenever the vicious portion of population shall be permitted to gather in bands of hundreds and thousands, and burn churches, ravage and rob provision-stores, throw printing-presses into rivers, shoot editors, and hang and burn obnoxious persons at pleasure and with impunity, depend on it, this government cannot last. By such things the feelings of the best citizens will become more or less alienated from it, and thus it will be left without friends, or with too few, and those who are too weak to make their friendship effectual. At such a time, and under such circumstances, men of sufficient talent and ambition will not be wanting to seize the opportunity, strike the blow, and overturn that fair fabric which for the last half century has been the fondest hope of the lovers of freedom throughout the world.

I know the American people are much attached to their government; I know they would suffer much for its sake; I know they would endure evils long and patiently before they would ever think of exchanging it for another,—yet, notwithstanding all this, if the laws be continually disregarded and despised, if their rights to be secure in their persons and property are held by no better tenure than the caprice of a mob, the alienation of their affections from the government is the natural consequence; and to that sooner or later it must come.

Here, then, is one point from which danger must be expected.

The question recurs, "How shall we fortify against it?" The answer is simple. Let every American, every lover of liberty, every well-wisher to his posterity swear by the blood of the Revolution never to violate in the least particular the laws of the country, and never to tolerate their violation by others. As the patriots of seventy-six did to the support of the Declaration of Independence, and so to the support of the Constitution and laws, let every American pledge his life, his property, and his sacred honor—let every man remember that to violate the law is to trample on the blood of his father, and to tear the charter of his own and children's liberty. Let reverence for the laws be breathed by every American mother to the lisping babe that prattles on her lap; let it be taught in schools, in seminaries, and in colleges; let it be written in primers, in spelling-books, and in almanacs; let it be preached from the pulpit, proclaimed in legislative halls, and enforced in courts of justice. And, in short, let it become the political religion of the nation; and let the old and the young, the rich and poor, the grave and the gay of all sexes and tongues and colors sacrifice unceasingly upon its altars.

While ever a state of feeling such as this universally or even very generally prevails throughout the nation, vain will be every effort, and fruitless every attempt, to subvert our national freedom.

When I so pressingly urge a strict observance of all the laws, let me not be understood as saying that there are no bad laws, or that grievances may not arise for the redress for which no legal provisions have ever been made. I mean to say no such thing. But I do mean to say that although bad laws, if they exist, should be repealed as soon as possible, still, while they continue in force, for the sake of example they should be religiously observed. So also in unimproved cases. If such arise, let proper legal provisions be made for them with the least possible delay, but 'til then let them, if not too intolerable, be borne with.

There is no grievance that is a fit object of redress by mob law. In any case that may arise, as, for instance, the promulgation of abolitionism, one of two positions is necessarily true—that is, the thing is right within itself, therefore deserves the protection of all law and good citizens, or it is wrong, and therefore proper to be prohibited by legal enactments; and in neither case is the interposition of mob law either necessary, justifiable, or excusable.

But it may be asked, "Why suppose danger to our political institutions? Have we not preserved them for fifty years? And why may we not for fifty times as long?"

We hope there is no sufficient reason. We hope that all danger may be overcome; but to conclude that no danger may ever arise would itself be extremely dangerous. There are now, and will hereafter be, many causes, dangerous in their tendency, which have not existed heretofore, and which are not so insignificant as to merit attention. That our government should have been maintained in its original form, from its establishment until now, is not much to be wondered at. It had many props to support it through that period, which now are decayed and crumbled away. Through that period it was felt by all to be an undecided experiment; now it is understood to be a successful one. Then, all that sought celebrity and fame and distinction expected to find them in the success of that experiment. Their all was staked upon it; their destiny was inseparably linked with it. Their ambition aspired to display before an admiring world a practical demonstration of the truth of a proposition which had hitherto been considered at best no better than problematical—namely, the capability of a people to govern themselves. If they succeeded they were to be immortalized; their names were to be transferred to counties, and cities, and rivers, and mountains; and to be revered and sung, toasted through all time. If they failed, they were to be called knaves, and fools, and fanatics for a fleeting hour; then to sink and be forgotten. They succeeded. The experiment is successful, and thousands have won their deathless names in making it so. But the game is caught; I believe that the catching ends the pleasures of the chase. This field of glory is harvested, and the crop is already appropriated. But new reapers will arise, and they too will seek a field. It is to deny what the history of the world tells us is true, to suppose that men of ambition and talents will not continue to spring up amongst us. And when they do, they will as naturally seek the gratification of their ruling passion as others have done before them. The question then is, Can that gratification be found in supporting and maintaining an edifice that has been erected by others? Most certainly it cannot. Many great and good men, sufficiently qualified for any task they should undertake, may ever be found whose ambition would aspire to nothing beyond a seat in Congress, a gubernatorial or a presidential chair; but such belong not to the family of the lion, or the tribe of the eagle. What! think you these places would satisfy an Alexander, a Caesar, or a Napoleon? Never! Towering genius disdains a beaten path. It seeks regions hitherto unexplored. It sees no distinction in adding story to story upon the monuments of fame erected to the memory of others. It denies that it is a glory to serve under any chief. It scorns to tread in the footsteps of any predecessor, however illustrious. It thirsts and burns for distinction; and if possible, it will have it, whether at the expense of emancipating slaves or enslaving free men. Is it unreasonable, then, to expect that some man possessed of the loftiest genius, coupled with ambition to push it to its utmost stretch, will at some time spring up among us? And when such an one does, it will require the people to be united with each other, attached to the government and laws, and generally intelligent, to successfully frustrate his designs.

Distinction will be his paramount object, and although he would as willingly, perhaps more so, acquire it by doing good as harm, yet, that opportunity being past, and nothing left to be done in the way of building up, he would set boldly to the task of pulling down.

Here is a probable case, highly dangerous and such an one as could not well have existed heretofore.

Another reason which once was, but which to the same extent, is now no more, has done much in maintaining our institutions thus far. I mean the powerful influence which the interesting scenes of the Revolution had upon the passions of the people as distinguished from their judgment. By this influence the jealousy, the envy, and avarice incident to our nature, and so common to a state of peace, prosperity and conscious strength, were for the time in a great measure smothered and rendered inactive, while the deep-rooted principles of hate, the powerful motive of revenge, instead of being turned against each other, were directed exclusively against the British Nation. And thus, from the force of circumstances the basest principles of our nature were either made to lie dormant, or to become the active agents in the advancement of the noblest of causes—that of establishing and maintaining civil and religious liberty.

But this state of feeling must fade, is fading, has faded, with the circumstances that produced it.

I do not mean to say that the scenes of the Revolution are now or ever will be entirely forgotten, but that like everything else, they must fade from the memory of the world, and grow more and more dim by the lapse of time. In history, we hope, they will be read of, and recounted, so long as the Bible shall be read; but even granting that they will, their influence cannot be what it heretofore has been. Even they cannot be so universally known nor so vividly felt as they were by the generation just gone to rest. At the close of that struggle, nearly every adult male had been a participator in some of its scenes. The consequence was that of those scenes, in the form of a husband, a father, a son, or a brother, a living history was to be found in every family— a history bearing the indubitable testimonies of its own authenticity in the limbs mangled, in the scars of wounds received, in the midst of the very scenes related— a history, too, that could be read and understood alike by all, the wise and ignorant, the learned and the unlearned. But those histories are gone. They can be read no more forever. They were a fortress of strength; but what invading foemen could never do, the silent artillery of time has done—the leveling of its walls. They are gone. They were a forest of giant oaks; but the all-restless hurricane has swept over them, and left only here and there a lonely trunk despoiled of its verdure, shorn of its foliage, unshading and unshaded, to murmur in a few more gentle breezes, and to combat with mutilated limbs a few more rude storms and then to sink and be no more.

They were pillars of the temple of liberty; and now that they have crumbled away that temple must fall unless we, their descendants, supply their places with other pillars, hewn from the solid quarry of sober reason. Passion has helped us, but can do so no more. It will in future be our enemy. Reason— cold, calculating, unimpassioned reason—must furnish all the materials for our future support and defense. Let those materials be molded into general intelligence, sound morality, and, in particular, a reverence for the Constitution and laws; and that we improve to the last, that we remained free to the last, that we revered his name to the last, that during his long sleep we permitted no hostile foot to pass over or desecrate his resting-place, shall be that which, to learn, the last trumpet shall awaken our Washington.

Upon this let the proud fabric of freedom rest, as the rock of its basis; and as truly as it has been said of the only greater institution, "the gates of hell shall not prevail against it."

Words of Wisdom from the Lips of Lincoln

"Gold is good in its place; but loving, brave, patriotic men are better than gold."

"Would you undertake to disprove a proposition in Euclid by calling Euclid a liar?"

"I am like the boy that stumped his toe: hurt too much to laugh and too big to cry."

"Meet face to face and converse together—the best way to efface unpleasant feeling."

"I want it said of me that I plucked a thistle and planted a flower where I thought a flower would grow."

"Let not him who is homeless pull down the house of another, but let him labor diligently to build one for himself."

"You may fool all of the people some of the time, and some of the people all of the time, but you can not fool all of the people all of the time."

"If all that has been said in praise of woman were applied to the women of America, it would not do them justice . . . God bless the women of America!"

FIRST GREAT NATIONAL SPEECH OF LINCOLN

First Speech Delivered by Lincoln in the East, at Fifty-one Years of Age, before a
Great Mass Meeting at Cooper Union in New York City, on February 27, 1860—This
Is the Speech That First Made Lincoln a Great National Political Leader in America

MR. PRESIDENT AND FELLOW-CITIZENS OF NEW YORK: The facts with which I shall deal this evening are mainly old and familiar; nor is there anything new in the general use I shall make of them. If there shall be any novelty, it will be in the mode of presenting the facts, and the inferences and observations following that presentation. In his speech last autumn at Columbus, Ohio, as reported in the *New York Times*, Senator Douglas said:

Our fathers, when they framed the government under which we live, understood this question just as well, and even better, than we do now.

I fully indorse this, and I adopt it as a text for this discourse. I so adopt it because it furnishes a precise and an agreed starting-point for a discussion between Republicans and that wing of the Democracy headed by Senator Douglas. It simply leaves the inquiry: What was the understanding those fathers had of the question mentioned?

What is the frame of government under which we live? The answer must be, "The Constitution of the United States." That Constitution consists of the original, framed in 1787, and under which the present government first went into operation, and twelve subsequently framed amendments, the first ten of which were framed in 1789.

Who were our fathers that framed the Constitution? I suppose the "thirty-nine" who signed the original instrument may be fairly called our fathers who framed that part of the present government. It is almost exactly true to say they framed it, and it is altogether true to say they fairly represent the opinion and sentiment of the whole nation at that time. Their names, being familiar to nearly all, and accessible to quite all, need not now be repeated.

I take these "thirty-nine," for the present, as being "our fathers who framed the government under which we live." What is the question which, according to the test, those fathers understood "just as well, and even better, than we do now?"

It is this: Does the proper division of local from Federal authority, or anything in the Constitution, forbid our Federal government to control as to slavery in our Federal Territories?

Upon this, Senator Douglas holds the affirmative, and Republicans the negative. This affirmation and denial form an issue; and this issue—this question—is precisely what the text declares our fathers understood "better than we." Let us now inquire whether the "thirty-nine" or any of them ever acted upon this question; and if they did, how they acted upon it—how they expressed their better understanding. In 1784, three years before the Constitution, the United States, then owning the Northwestern Territory, and no other, the Congress of the Confederation had before them the question of prohibiting slavery in that Territory; and four of the "thirty-nine" who afterward framed the Constitution were in that Congress, and voted on that question. Of these, Roger Sherman, Thomas Mifflin, and Hugh Williamson voted for the prohibition, thus showing that, in their understanding, no line dividing local from Federal authority, nor anything else, properly forbade the Federal

Federal Control Is a Principle of the Government

Government to control as to slavery in Federal territory. The other of the four, James McHenry, voted against the prohibition, showing that for some cause he thought it improper to vote for it.

In 1787, still before the Constitution, but while the convention was in session framing it, and while the Northwestern Territory still was the only Territory owned by the United States, the same question of prohibiting slavery in the Territory again came before the Congress of the Confederation; and two more of the "thirty-nine" who afterward signed the Constitution were in that Congress, and voted on the question. They were William Blount and William Few; and they both voted for the prohibition—thus showing that in their understanding no line divided local from Federal authority, nor anything else, properly forbade the Federal Government to control as to slavery in Federal territory. This time prohibition became a law, being part of what is now well known as the ordinance of '87.

The question of Federal control of slavery in the Territories seems not to have been directly before the convention which framed the original Constitution; and hence it is not recorded that the "thirty-nine" or any of them, while engaged on that instrument, expressed any opinion on that precise question.

In 1789, by the first Congress which sat under the Constitution, an act was passed to enforce the ordinance of '87, including the prohibition of slavery in the Northwestern Territory. The bill for this act was reported by one of the "thirty-nine"—Thomas Fitzsimmons, then a member of the House of Representatives from Pennsylvania. It went through all its stages without a word of opposition, and finally passed both branches without ayes and nays, which is equivalent to a unanimous passage. In this Congress, there were sixteen of the "thirty-nine" fathers who framed the original Constitution. They were John Langdon, Nicholas Gilman, William S. Johnson, Roger Sherman, Robert Morris, Thomas Fitzsimmons, William Few, Abraham Baldwin, Rufus King, William Paterson, George Clymer, Richard Bassett, George Read, Pierce Butler, Daniel Carrol and James Madison.

This shows that, in their understanding, no line dividing local from Federal authority, nor anything in the Constitution, properly forbade Congress to prohibit slavery in the Federal Territory; else both their fidelity to correct principle, and their oath to support the Constitution, would have constrained them to oppose the prohibition.

Again, George Washington, another of the "thirty-nine," was then President of the United States, and as such approved and signed the bill, thus completing its validity as a law, and thus showing that, in his understanding, no line dividing local from Federal authority, nor anything in the Constitution, forbade the Federal Government to control as to slavery in Federal territory.

No great while after the adoption of the original Constitution, North Carolina ceded to the Federal Government the country now constituting the State of Tennessee; and a few years later Georgia ceded that which now constitutes the States of Mississippi and Alabama. In both deeds of cession it was made a condition by the ceding States that the Federal Government should not prohibit slavery in the ceded country. Besides this, slavery was then actually in the ceded country. Under these circumstances, Congress, on taking charge of these countries, did not absolutely prohibit slavery within them. But they did interfere with it—take control of it—even there, to a certain extent. In

1798, Congress organized the Territory of Mississippi. In the act of organization, they prohibited the bringing of slaves into the Territory from any place without the United States, by fine, and giving freedom to slaves so brought. This act passed both branches of Congress without yeas and nays. In that Congress, there were three of the "thirty-nine" who framed the original Constitution. They were John Langdon, George Read and Abraham Baldwin. They all probably voted for it. Certainly they would have placed their opposition to it upon record if, in their understanding, any line dividing local from Federal authority, or anything in the Constitution, properly forbade the Federal Government to control as to slavery in Federal territory.

In 1803, the Federal Government purchased the Louisiana country. Our former territorial acquisitions came from certain of our States; but this Louisiana country was acquired from a foreign nation. In 1804, Congress gave a territorial organization to that part of it which now constitutes the State of Louisiana. New Orleans, lying within that part, was an old and comparatively large city. There were other considerable towns and settlements, and slavery was extensively and thoroughly intermingled with the people. Congress did not, in the Territorial Act, prohibit slavery; but they did interfere with it—take control of it—in a more marked and extensive way than they did in the case of Mississippi. The substance of the provision therein made in relation to slaves was:

1st. That no slave should be imported into the Territory from foreign parts.

2nd. That no slave should be carried into it who had been imported into the United States since the first day of May, 1798.

That no slave should be carried into it, except by the owner, and for his own use as a settler; the penalty in all these cases being a fine upon the violator of the law, and freedom to the slave.

This act also was passed without ayes or nays. In the Congress which passed it there were two of the "thirty-nine." They were Abraham Baldwin and Jonathan Dayton. As stated in the case of Mississippi, it is probable they both voted for it. They would not have allowed it to pass without recording their opposition to it if, in their understanding, it violated either the line properly dividing local from Federal authority, or any provision of the Constitution.

In 1819-20 came and passed the Missouri question. Many votes were taken, by yeas and nays, in both branches of Congress, upon the various phases of the general question. Two of the "thirty-nine"—Rufus King and Charles Pinckney—were members of that Congress. Mr. King steadily voted for slavery prohibition and against all compromises, while Mr. Pinckney as steadily voted against slavery prohibition and against all compromises. By this, Mr. King showed that, in his understanding, no line dividing local from Federal authority, nor anything in the Constitution, was violated by Congress prohibiting slavery in Federal territory; while Mr. Pinckney, by his votes, showed that, in his understanding, there was some sufficient reason for opposing such prohibition in that case.

The cases I have mentioned are the only acts of the "thirty-nine," or of any of them, upon the direct issue, which I have been able to discover.

To enumerate, the persons who thus acted as being four in 1784, two in 1787, seventeen in 1789, three in 1798, two in 1804, and two in 1819-20, there would be thirty of them. But this would be counting John Langdon, Roger Sherman, William Few, Rufus King, and George Read each twice, and Abraham Baldwin three times. The true number of those of the "thirty-nine" whom I have shown to have acted upon the question which, by the text, they understood better than we, is twenty-three, leaving sixteen not shown to have acted upon it in any way.

Here, then, we have twenty-three out of our "thirty-nine" fathers "who framed the government under which we live," who have, upon their official responsibility and their corporal oaths, acted upon the very question which the text affirms they "understood just as well, and even better, than we do now"; and twenty-one of them—a clear majority of the whole "thirty-nine"— so acting upon it as to make them guilty of gross political impropriety and willful perjury if, in their understanding, any proper division between local and Federal authority, or anything in the Constitution they had made themselves, and sworn to support, forbade the Federal Government to control as to slavery in the Federal Territories. Thus the twenty-one acted; and, as actions speak louder than words, so actions under such responsibility speak still louder.

Two of the twenty-three voted against congressional prohibition of slavery in the Federal Territories, in the instances in which they acted upon the question. But for what reasons they so voted is not known. They may have done so because they thought a proper division of local from Federal authority, or some provision or principle of the Constitution, stood in the way; or they may, without any such question, have voted against the prohibition on what appeared to them to be sufficient grounds for expediency. No one who has sworn to support the Constitution can conscientiously vote for what he understands to be an unconstitutional measure, however expedient he may think it; but one may and ought to vote against a measure which he thinks constitutional if, at the time, he deems it inexpedient. It, therefore, would be unsafe to set down even the two who voted against the prohibition as having done so because, in their understanding, any proper division of local from Federal authority, or anything in the Constitution, that forbade the Federal Government to control as to slavery in Federal territory.

The remaining sixteen of the "thirty-nine," so far as I discovered, have left no record of their understanding upon the direct question of Federal control of slavery in the Federal Territories. But there is much reason to believe that their understanding upon that question would not have appeared different from that of their twenty-three compeers, had it been manifested at all.

For the purpose of adhering rigidly to the text, I have purposely omitted whatever understanding may have been manifested by any person, however distinguished, other than the "thirty-nine" fathers who framed the original Constitution; and, for the same reason, I have also omitted whatever understanding may have been manifested by any of the "thirty-nine," even on any other phase of the general question of slavery. If we should look into their acts and declarations on those other phases, as the foreign slave-trade, and the morality and policy of slavery generally, it would appear to us that on the direct question of Federal control of slavery in Federal Territories, the sixteen, if they had acted at all would probably have acted just as the twenty-three did. Among that sixteen were several of the most noted anti-slavery men of those times,—as Dr. Franklin, Alexander Hamilton, and Gouverneur Morris,—while there was not one now known to be otherwise, unless it may be John Rutledge, of South Carolina.

The sum of the whole is that of our "thirty-nine" fathers who framed the original Constitution, twenty-one—a clear majority of the whole—certainly understood that no proper division of local from Federal authority, nor any part of the Constitution, forbade the Federal Government to control slavery in the Federal Territories; while all the rest had probably the same understanding. Such, unquestionably, was the understanding of our fathers who framed the original Constitution; and the text affirms that they understood the question "better than we."

But, so far, I have been considering the understanding of the question manifested by the framers of the original Constitution. In and by the original instrument, a mode was provided for amending it; and, as I have already stated, the present frame of "the government under which we live" consists of that original, and twelve amendatory articles, and not in the original instrument. Those who now insist that Federal control of slavery in Federal Territories violates the Constitution, point us to the provisions which they suppose it thus violates; and, as I understand, they all fix upon provisions in these amendatory articles, and not in the original instrument. The Supreme Court, in the Dred Scott case, plant themselves upon the fifth amendment, which provides that no person shall be deprived of "life, liberty, or property, without the due process of law"; while Senator Douglas and his peculiar adherents plant themselves upon the Tenth Amendment, provided that "the powers not delegated to the United States by the Constitution" "are reserved to the States respectively, or to the people."

Now, it so happens that these amendments were framed by the first Congress which sat under the Constitution—the identical Congress which passed the act, already mentioned, enforcing the prohibition of slavery in the North-western Territory. Not only was it the same Congress, but they were the very identical, same individual men who, at the same session, and at the same time within the session, had under consideration, and in progress toward maturity, these constitutional amendments, and this act prohibiting slavery in all the territory the nation then owned. The constitutional amendments were introduced before, and passed after, the act of enforcing the ordinance of '87; so that, during the whole pendency of the act to enforce the ordinance, the constitutional amendments were also pending.

The seventy-six members of that Congress, including sixteen of the framers of the original Constitution, as before stated, were pre-eminently our fathers who framed that part of "the government under which we live" which is now claimed as forbidding the Federal Government to control slavery in the Federal Territories.

Is it not a little presumptuous in anyone at this day to affirm that the two things which that Congress deliberately framed, and carried to maturity at the same time, are absolutely inconsistent with each other? And does not such affirmation become impudently absurd when coupled with the other affirmation, from the same mouth, that those who did the two things alleged to be inconsistent, understood whether they really were inconsistent better than we—better than he who affirms that they are inconsistent?

Honest Conviction Is the Inherent Right of Man

It is surely safe to assume that the thirty-nine framers of the original Constitution, and the seventy-six members of the Congress which framed the amendments thereto, taken together, do certainly include those who may be fairly called "our fathers who framed the government under which we live." And so assuming, I defy any man to show that any one of them ever, in his whole life, declared that, in his understanding, any proper division of local from Federal authority, or any part of the Constitution, forbade the Federal Government to control as to slavery in the Federal Territories. I go a step further. I defy anyone to show that any living man in the whole world ever did, prior to the beginning of the present century (and I might almost say prior to the beginning of the last half century) declare that, in his understanding, any proper division of local from Federal authority, or any part of the Constitution, forbade the Federal Government to control as to slavery in the Federal Territories. To those who now so declare I give not only "our fathers who framed the government under which we live," but with them all other living men within the century in which it was framed, among whom to search, and they shall not be able to find the evidence of a single man agreeing with them.

Now, and here, let me guard a little against being misunderstood. I do not mean to say we are bound to follow implicitly in whatever our fathers did. To do so would be to discard all the lights of current experience—to reject all progress, all improvement. What I do say is that if we would supplant the opinions and policy of our fathers in any case, we should do so upon evidence so conclusive, and argument so clear, that even their great authority, fairly considered and weighed, cannot stand; and most surely not in a case whereof we ourselves declare they understood the question better than we.

If any man at this day sincerely believes that a proper division of local from Federal authority, or any part of the Constitution, forbids the Federal Government to control as to slavery in the Federal Territories, he is right to say so, and to enforce his position by truthful evidence and fair argument which he can. But he has no right to mislead others, who have less access to history, and less leisure to study it, into the false belief that "our fathers who framed the government under which we live" were of the same opinion—thus substituting falsehood and deception for truthful evidence and fair argument. If any man at this day sincerely believes "our fathers who framed the government under which we live" used and applied principles, in other cases, which ought to have led them to understand that a proper division of local from Federal authority, or some part of the Constitution, forbids the Federal Government to control as to slavery in the Federal Territories, he is right to say so. But he should, at the same time, brave the responsibility of declaring that in his opinion, he understands their principles better than they did themselves; and especially should he not shirk that responsibility by asserting that they "understood the question as well, and even better, than we do now."

But enough! Let all who believe that "our fathers who framed the government under which we live understood this question just as well, and even better, than we do now," speak as they spoke, and act as they acted upon it. This is all Republicans ask—all Republicans desire—in relation to slavery. As those fathers marked it, so let it be again marked, as an evil not to be extended, but to be tolerated and protected only because of and so far as its actual presence among us makes that toleration and protection a necessity. Let all the guarantees those fathers gave it be not grudgingly, but fully and fairly, maintained. For this Republicans contend, and with this, so far as I know or believe, they will be content.

And now, if they would listen,—as I suppose they will not—I would address a few words to the Southern people.

I would say to them: You consider yourselves a reasonable and a just people; and I consider that in the general qualities of reason and justice you are not inferior to any other people. Still, when you speak of us Republicans, you do so only to denounce us as reptiles, or, at the best, as no better than outlaws. You will grant a hearing to pirates or murderers, but nothing like it to "Black Republicans." In all your contentions with one another, each of you deem an unconditional condemnation of "Black Republicanism" as the first thing to be attended to. Indeed, such condemnation of us seems to be an indispensable prerequisite—license so to speak—among you to be admitted or permitted to speak at all. Now can you or not be prevailed upon to pause and to consider whether this is quite just to us, or even to yourselves? Bring forward your charges and specifications, and then be patient long enough to hear us deny or justify.

You say we are sectional. We deny it. That makes an issue; and the burden of proof is upon you. You produce your proof; and what is it? Why, that our party has no existence in your section—gets no votes in your section. The fact is substantially true; but does it prove the issue? If it does, then in case we should, without change of principle, begin to get votes in your section, we should thereby cease to be sectional. You cannot escape this conclusion; and yet, are you willing to abide by it? If you are, you will probably soon find that we have ceased to be sectional, for we shall get votes in your section this very year. You will then begin to discover, as the truth plainly is, that your proof does not touch the issue. The fact that we get no votes in your section is a fact of your making, and not of ours. And if there be fault in that fact, that fault is primarily yours, and remains so until you show that we repel you by some wrong principle or practice. If we do repel you by any wrong principle or practice, the fault is ours; but this brings you to where you ought to have started—a discussion of the right or wrong of our principle. If our principle, put in practice, would wrong your section for the benefit of ours, or for any other object, then our principle and we with it are sectional, and are justly opposed and denounced as such. Meet us, then, on the question of whether our principle, put in practice, would wrong your section; and so meet us if it were possible that something may be said on our side. Do you accept the challenge? No! Then you really believe that the principle which "our fathers who framed the government under which we live" thought so clearly right as to adopt it, and indorse it again and again, upon their official oaths, is in fact so clearly wrong as to demand your condemnation without a moment's consideration.

Some of you delight to flaunt in our faces the warning against sectional parties given by Washington in his Farewell Address. Less than eight years before Washington gave that warning, he had, as President of the United States, approved and signed an act of Congress enforcing the prohibition of slavery in the Northwest Territory, which act embodied the policy of the government upon that subject up to and at the very moment he penned that warning; and about a year after he penned it, he wrote Lafayette that he considered that prohibition a wise measure, expressing in the same connection his hope that we should at some time have a confederacy of free States.

Bearing this in mind, and seeing that sectionalism has since arisen upon this same subject, is that warning a weapon in your hands against us, or in our hands against you? Could Washington himself speak, would he cast the blame of that sectionalism upon us, who sustain his policy, or upon you, who repudiate it? We respect that warning of Washington, and we commend it to you, together with his example pointing to the right application of it.

But you say you are conservative—eminently conservative—while we are revolutionary, destructive, or something of the sort. What is conservatism? Is it not adherence to the old and tried, against the new and untried? We stick to, contend for, the identical old policy on the point in controversy which was adopted by "our fathers who framed the government under which we live"; while you with one accord reject, and scout, nd spit upon that old policy, and insist upon substituting something new. True, you disagree among yourselves as to what that substitute shall be. You are divided on new propositions and plans, but you are unanimous in rejecting and denouncing the old policy of the fathers. Some of you are for reviving the foreign slave-trade; some for a congressional slave code for the Territories; some for Congress forbidding the Territories to prohibit slavery within their limits; some for maintaining slavery in the Territories through the judiciary; some for the "gur-reat pur-rinciple" that "if one man would enslave another, no third man should object," fantastically called "popular sovereignty"; but never a man among you is in favor of Federal prohibition of slavery in Federal Territories, according to the practice of "our fathers who framed the government under which we live." Not one of all your various plans can show a precedent or an advocate in the century within which our government originated. Consider, then, whether your claim of conservatism for yourselves, and your charge of destructiveness against us, are based on the most clear and stable foundations.

Again, you say we have made the slavery question more prominent than it formerly was. We deny it. We admit that it is more prominent, but we deny that we made it so. It was not we, but you, who discarded the old policy of the fathers. We resisted, and still resist, your innovation; and thence comes the greater prominence of the question. Would you have that question reduced to its former proportions? Go back to that old policy. What has been will be again, under the same conditions. If you would have the peace of the old times, re-adopt the precepts and policy of the old times.

You charge that we stir up insurrections among your slaves. We deny it; and what is your proof? Harper's Ferry! John Brown! John Brown was no Republican; and you have failed to implicate a single Republican in his Harper's Ferry enterprise. If any member of our party is guilty in that matter, you know it, or you do not know it. If you do know it, you are inexcusable for not designating the man and proving the fact. If you do not know it, you are inexcusable for asserting it, and especially for persisting in the assertion after you have tried and failed to make the proof. You need not be told that persisting in a charge which one does not know to be true, is simply malicious slander.

New Political Parties Are Always Called Radical

Some of you admit that no Republican designedly aided or encouraged the Harper's Ferry affair, but still insist that our doctrines and declarations necessarily lead to such results. We do not believe it. We know we hold no doctrine, and make no declaration, which were not held to and made by "our fathers who framed the government under which we live." You never dealt fairly by us in relation to this affair. When it occurred, some important State elections were near at hand, and you were in evident glee with the belief that, by charging the blame upon us, you could get an advantage of us in those elections. The elections came and your expectations were not quite fulfilled. Every Republican man knew that, as to himself at least, your charge was a slander, and he was not much inclined by it to cast his vote in your favor. Republican doctrines and declarations are accompanied with a continual protest against any interference whatever with your slaves, or with you about your slaves. Surely, this does not encourage them to revolt. True, we do, in common with "our fathers who framed the government under which we live," declare our belief that slavery is wrong; but the slaves do not hear us declare even this. For anything we say or do, the slaves would scarcely know that there is a Republican party. I believe they would not, in fact, generally know it but for your misrepresentations of us in their hearing. In your political contests among yourselves, each faction charges the other with sympathy with Black Republicanism; and then, to give point to the charge, defines Black Republicanism to simply be insurrection, blood and thunder among the slaves.

Slave insurrections are no more common now than they were before the Republican party was organized. What induced the Southampton insurrection, twenty-eight years ago, in which at least three times as many lives were lost as at Harper's Ferry? You can scarcely stretch your very elastic fancy to the conclusion that Southampton was "got up by Black Republicanism." In the present state of things in the United States, I do not think a general, or even a very extensive, slave insurrection is possible. The indispensable concert of action cannot be attained. The slaves have no means of rapid communication; nor can incendiary freemen, black or white, supply it. The explosive materials are everywhere in parcels; but there neither are, nor can be supplied, the indispensable connecting trains.

Much is said by Southern people about the affection of slaves for their masters and mistresses; and a part of it, at least, is true. A plot for an uprising could scarcely be devised and communicated to twenty individuals before some one of them, to save the life of a favorite master or mistress, would divulge it. This is the rule; and the slave revolution in Hayti was not an exception to it, but a case occurring under peculiar circumstances. The gunpowder plot of English history, though not connected with slaves, was more in point. In that case only about twenty were admitted to the secret; and yet one of them in his anxiety to save a friend, betrayed the plot to that friend, and, by consequences, averted that calamity. Occasional poisonings from the kitchen, and open or stealthy assassinations in the field, and local revolts extending to a score or so, will continue to occur as the natural results of slavery; but no general insurrection of slaves, as I think, can happen in this country for a long time. Whoever much fears, or much hopes, for such an event, will be alike disappointed.

A People's Hopes May Be Restrained—Never Destroyed

In the language of Mr. Jefferson, uttered many years ago, "It is still **in** our power to direct the process of emancipation and deportation peaceably, and in such slow degrees as that the evil will wear off insensibly; and their places be, *pari passu*, filled up by white laborers. If, on the contrary, it is left to force itself on, human nature must shudder at the prospect held up."

Mr. Jefferson did not seem to say, nor do I, that the power of emancipation is in the Federal Government. He spoke of Virginia; and, as to the power of emancipation, I speak of the slave-holding States only. The Federal Government, however, as we insist, has the power of restraining the extension of the institution—the power to insure that a slave insurrection shall never occur on any American soil which is now free from slavery.

John Brown's effort was peculiar. It was not a slave insurrection. It was an attempt by white men to get up a revolt among slaves, in which the slaves refused to participate. In fact, it was so absurd that the slaves, with all their ignorance, saw plainly enough it could not succeed. That affair, in its philosophy, corresponds with the many attempts, related in history, at the assassination of kings and emperors. An enthusiast broods over the oppression of a people till he fancies himself commissioned by Heaven to liberate them. He ventures the attempt, which ends in little less than his own execution. Orsini's attempt on Louis Napoleon, and John Brown's attempt at Harper's Ferry, were, in their philosophy, precisely the same. The eagerness to cast blame on Old England in the one case, and on New England in the other, does not disprove the sameness of the two things.

And how much would it avail you, if you could, by the use of John Brown, Helper's Book, and the like, break up the Republican organization? Human action can be modified to some extent, but human nature cannot be changed. There is a judgment and a feeling against slavery in this nation, which cast at least a million and a half votes. You cannot destroy that judgment and feeling—that sentiment—by breaking up the political organization which rallies around it. You can scarcely scatter and disperse an army which has been formed into order in the face of your heaviest fire; but if you could, how much would you gain by forcing the sentiment which created it out of the peaceful channel of the ballot-box into some other channel. What would that other channel probably be? Would the number of John Browns be lessened or enlarged by the operation?

But you will break up the Union rather than submit to a denial of your constitutional rights.

That has a somewhat reckless sound; but it would be palliated, if not fully justified, were we proposing, by the mere force of numbers, to deprive you of some right plainly written down in the Constitution. But we are proposing no such thing.

When you make these declarations you have a specific and well understood allusion to an assumed constitutional right of yours to take slaves into the Federal Territories, and to hold them there as property. But no such right is specifically written in the Constitution. That instrument is literally silent about any such right. We, on the contrary, deny that such a right exists in the Constitution, even by implication.

Your purpose, then, plainly stated, is that you will destroy the government,

Rule or Ruin Is Not a Principle of Self-Government

unless you be allowed to construe and force the Constitution as you please, on all points in dispute between you and us. You will rule or ruin in all events.

This, plainly stated, is your language. Perhaps you will say the Supreme Court has decided the disputed and constitutional question in your favor. Not quite so. But waiving the lawyer's distinction between dictum and decision, the court has decided the question for you in a sort of way. The court has substantially said, it is your constitutional right to take slaves into the Federal Territories, and to hold them there as property. When I say the decision was made in a sort of way, I mean it was made in a divided court, by a bare majority of the judges, and they not quite agreeing with one another in the reasons for making it; that it is so made as that its avowed supporters disagree with one another about its meaning, and that it was mainly based upon a mistaken statement of fact—the statement in the opinion that "the right of property in a slave is distinctly and expressly affirmed in the Constitution."

An inspection of the Constitution will show that the right of property in a slave is not "distinctly and expressly affirmed" in it. Bear in mind, the judges do not pledge their judicial opinion that such right is impliedly affirmed in the Constitution; but they pledge their veracity, that it is "distinctly and expressly" affirmed there—"distinctly," that is, not mingled with anything else—"expressly," that is, in words meaning just that, without the aid of any inference, and susceptible of no other meaning.

If they had only pledged their judicial opinion that such right is affirmed in the instrument by implication, it would be open to others to show that neither the word "slave" nor "slavery" is to be found in the Constitution, nor the word "property" even, in any connection with language alluding to the things slaves or slavery; and that wherever in that instrument the slave is alluded to, he is called a "person"; and wherever his master's legal right in relation to him is alluded to, it is spoken of as "service or labor which may be due"—as a debt payable in service or labor. Also it would be open to show, by contemporaneous history, that this mode of alluding to slaves and slavery, instead of speaking of them, was employed on purpose to exclude from the Constitution the idea that there could be property in man.

To show all this is easy and certain:

When this obvious mistake of the judges shall be brought to their notice, is it not reasonable to expect that they will withdraw the mistaken statement, and reconsider the conclusion based upon it?

And then it is to be remembered that "our fathers who framed the government under which we live"—the men who made the Constitution—decided this same constitutional question in our favor long ago; decided it without division among themselves when making the decision; without division among themselves; without the meaning of it after it was made, and, so far as any evidence is left, without basing it upon any mistaken statement of facts.

Under all these circumstances, do you really feel yourselves justified to break up this government unless such a court decision as yours is shall be at once submitted to as a conclusive and final rule of political action? But you will not abide the election of a Republican president! In that supposed event, you say, you will destroy the Union; and then, you say, the great crime of having destroyed it will be upon us! That is cool. A highwayman holds a pistol to my ear, and mutters through his teeth, "Stand and deliver, or I shall kill you, and then you will be a murderer!"

To be sure, what the robber demanded of me—my money—was my own; and I had a clear right to keep it; but it was no more my own than my vote is my own; and the threat of death to me, to extort my money, and the threat of destruction to the Union, to extort my vote, can scarcely be distinguished in principle.

A few words now to Republicans. It is exceedingly desirable that all parts of this great Confederacy shall be at peace, and in harmony one with another. Let us Republicans do our part to have it so. Even though much provoked, let us do nothing through passion and ill temper. Even though the Southern people will not so much as listen to us, let us calmly consider their demands, and yield to them if, in our deliberate view of duty, we possibly can. Judging by all they say and do, and by the subject and nature of their controversy with us, let us determine, if we can, what will satisfy them.

Will they be satisfied if the Territories be unconditionally surrendered to them? We know they will not. In all their present complaints against us, the Territories are scarcely mentioned. Invasions and insurrections are the rage now. Will it satisfy them, if, in the future, we have nothing to do with invasions and insurrections? We know it will not. We so know, because we know we never had anything to do with invasions and insurrections; and yet this total abstaining does not exempt us from the charge and the denunciation.

The question recurs what will satisfy them? Simply this: We must not only let them alone, but we must somehow convince them that we do let them alone. This, we know by experience, is no easy task. We have been so trying to convince them from the beginning of our organization, but with no success. In all our platforms and speeches we have constantly protested our purpose to let them alone; but this has had no tendency to convince them. Alike unavailing to convince them is the fact that they have never detected a man of us in any attempt to disturb them.

These natural and apparently adequate means all failing, what will convince them? This, and this only: Cease to call slavery wrong, and join them in calling it right. And this must be done thoroughly—done in acts as well as in words. Silence will not be tolerated—we must place ourselves avowedly with them. Senator Douglas's new sedition law must be enacted and enforced, suppressing all declarations that slavery is wrong, whether made in politics, in presses, in pulpits, or in private. We must arrest and return their fugitive slaves with greedy pleasure. We must pull down our free-State constitutions. The whole atmosphere must be disinfected from all taint of opposition to slavery, before they will cease to believe that all their troubles proceed from us.

I am quite aware they do not state their case precisely in this way. Most of them would probably say to us, "Let us alone; do nothing to us, and say what you please about slavery." But we do let them alone, I have never disturbed them,—so that, after all, it is what we say which dissatisfies them. They will continue to accuse us of doing, until we cease saying.

I am also aware that they have not as yet in terms demanded the overthrow of our free-State constitutions. Yet these constitutions declare the wrong of slavery with more solemn emphasis than do all other sayings against

Let Us Dare to Do Our Duty as We Understand It

it; and, when all these other sayings have been silenced, the overthrow of these constitutions will be demanded, and nothing be left to resist the demand. It is nothing to the contrary that they do not demand the whole of this just now. Demanding what they do, and for the reason they do, they can voluntarily stop nowhere short of this consummation. Holding, as they do, that slavery is morally right and socially elevating, they cannot cease to demand a full national recognition of it as a legal right and social blessing.

Nor can we justifiably withhold this on any ground save our conviction that slavery is wrong. If slavery is right, all words, acts, laws, and constitutions against it are themselves wrong, and should be silenced and swept away. If it is right, we cannot justly object to its nationality—its universality; if it is wrong, they cannot justly insist upon its extension—its enlargement. All they ask we could readily grant, if we thought slavery right; all we ask they could as readily grant, if they thought it wrong. Their thinking it right and our thinking it wrong is the precise fact upon which depends the whole controversy. Thinking it right, as they do, they are not to blame for desiring its full recognition as being right; but thinking it wrong as we do, can we yield to them? Can we cast our votes with their view, and against our own? In view of our moral, social, and political responsibilities, can we do this?

Wrong as we think slavery is, we can yet afford to let it alone where it is, because that much is due to the necessity arising from its actual presence in the nation; but can we, while our votes will prevent it, allow it to spread into the national Territories, and to overrun us here in these free States? If our sense of duty forbids this, then let us stand by our duty fearlessly and effectively. Let us be diverted by none of those sophistical contrivances wherewith we are so industriously plied and belabored—contrivances such as groping for some middle ground between the right and the wrong: vain as the search for a man who should be neither a living man nor a dead man; such as a policy of "don't care" on a question about which all true men do care; such as Union appeals beseeching true Union men to yield to Disunionists, reversing the divine rule, and calling, not the sinners, but the righteous to repentance; such as invocations to Washington, imploring men to unsay what Washington said and undo what Washington did.

Neither let us be slandered from our duty by false accusations against us, nor frightened from it by menaces of destruction to the government, nor of dungeons to ourselves. Let us have faith that right makes might, and in that faith let us dare to do our duty as we understand it.

"Be sure you put your feet in the right place, then stand firm."
"When you have written a wrathful letter—*put it in the stove!*"
"Suspicion and jealousy never did help any man in any situation."
"Never get between the woman's skillet and the man's axhelve."
"Shakespeare was the best judge of human nature that ever wrote."
"It is better only sometimes to be right than at all times to be wrong."
"If men never began to drink they would never become drunkards."
"Don't shoot too high—aim low and the common people will understand."
"I do not think much of a man who is not wiser today than he was yesterday."

SPEECHES IN LINCOLN'S POLITICAL GREATNESS

Lincoln's Speech in Accepting Nomination for President of the United States at His Home in Springfield, Illinois, May 19, 1860, at Fifty-one Years of Age

MR. CHAIRMAN AND GENTLEMEN OF THE COMMITTEE: I tender to you, and through you to the Republican National Convention, and all the people represented in it, my profoundest thanks for the high honor done me, which you now formally announce.

Deeply, and even painfully sensible of the great responsibility which is inseparable from this high honor—a responsibility which I could almost wish had fallen upon some one of the far more eminent men and experienced statesmen whose distinguished names were before the convention—I shall, by your leave, consider more fully the resolutions of the convention, denominated the platform, and without any unnecessary or unreasonable delay respond to you, Mr. Chairman, in writing, not doubting that the platform will be found satisfactory, and the nomination gratefully accepted.

And now I will not longer defer the pleasure of taking you, and each of you, by the hand.

Lincoln's Last Speech to His Neighbors When Leaving His Home at Springfield, Illinois, on February 11, 1861, to Go to the White House at Washington

MY FRIENDS: No one, not in my situation, can appreciate my feeling of sadness at this parting. To this place, and the kindness of these people, I owe everything. Here I have lived a quarter of a century, and have passed from a young to an old man. Here my children have been born, and one is buried. I now leave, not knowing when or whether ever I may return, with a task before me greater than that which rested upon Washington. Without the assistance of that Divine Being who ever attended him, I cannot succeed. With that assistance, I cannot fail. Trusting in Him who can go with me, and remain with you, and be everywhere for good, let us confidently hope that all will yet be well. To His care commending you, as I hope in your prayers you will commend me, I bid you an affectionate farewell.

Lincoln's Speech at Independence Hall in Philadelphia at a Flag Raising on Washington's Birthday, February 22, 1861, on His Way to the National Capital

FELLOW-CITIZENS: I am invited and called before you to participate in raising above Independence Hall the flag of our country, with an additional star upon it! I propose now to say that when the flag was originally raised here, it had but thirteen stars. I wish to call your attention to the fact that, under the blessing of God, each additional star has given additional prosperity and happiness to this country, until it has advanced to its present condition; and its welfare in the future, as well as in the past, is in your hands. Cultivating the spirit that animated our fathers, who gave renown and celebrity to this Hall, cherishing that fraternal feeling which has so long characterized us as a nation, excluding passion, ill temper, and precipitate action on all occasions, I think we may promise ourselves that not only the new star placed upon that flag shall be permitted to remain there to our permanent prosperity for years to come, but additional ones shall from time to time be placed there until we shall number, as it was anticipated by the great historian, five hundred millions of happy and prosperous people.

With these few remarks, I proceed to the very agreeable duty assigned to me.

SPEECH THAT MOLDED A NATION'S FUTURE

Great Epoch-Making Address Delivered by Abraham Lincoln as He Took the
Oath of Allegiance on His First Inauguration as President of the United States
Before a Vast Throng at the National Capitol on the Fourth of March in 1861

FELLOW-CITIZENS OF THE UNITED STATES: In com-
pliance with a custom as old as the government itself, I appear before you to address you briefly, and to take in your presence the
oath prescribed by the Constitution of the United States to be
taken by the President "before he enters the execution of his office."
I do not consider it necessary at present for me to discuss those matters
of administration about which there is no special anxiety or excitement.

Apprehension seems to exist among the people of the Southern States that
by the accession of a Republican administration their property and their peace
and personal security are to be endangered. There has never been any reasonable cause for such apprehension. Indeed, the most ample evidence to the
contrary has all the while existed and been open to their inspection. It is
found in nearly all the published speeches of him who now addresses you. I
do but quote from one of those speeches when I declare that "I have no purpose,
directly or indirectly, to interfere with the institution of slavery in the States
where it exists. I believe I have no lawful right to do so, and I have no
inclination to do so." Those who nominated and elected me did so with full
knowledge that I had made this and many similar declarations, and had never
recanted them. And, more than this, they placed in the platform for my accept-
ance, and as a law to themselves and to me, the clear and emphatic resolution
which I now read:

RESOLVED: That the maintenance inviolate of the rights of the States, and
especially the right of each State to order and control its own domestic institutions according to its own judgment exclusively, is essential to that balance of power on which the
perfection and endurance of our political fabric depend, and we denounce the lawless
invasion by armed force of the soil of any State or Territory, no matter under what pretext,
as among the greatest of crimes.

I now reiterate these sentiments; and, in doing so, I only press upon the
public attention the most conclusive evidence of which the case is susceptible,
that the property, peace, and security of no section are to be in any wise endangered by the now incoming administration. I add, too, that all the protection
which, consistently with the Constitution and the laws, can be given, will be
cheerfully given to all the States when lawfully demanded, for whatever cause—
as cheerfully to one section as to another.

There is much controversy about the delivering up of fugitives from service
or labor. The clause I now read is as plainly written in the Constitution as
any other of its provisions:

No person held to service or labor in one State, under the laws thereof, escaping into
another, shall in consequence of any law or regulation therein be discharged from such
service or labor, but shall be delivered up on claim of the party to whom such service or
labor may be due.

It is scarcely questioned that this provision was intended by those who
made it for the reclaiming of what we call fugitive slaves; and the intention
of the law giver is the law. All members of Congress swear their support to
the whole Constitution—to this provision as to any other. To the proposition,
then, that slaves whose cases come within the terms of this clause "shall be
delivered up," their oaths are unanimous. Now, if they would make the effort

in good temper, could they not with nearly equal unanimity frame and pass a law by means of which to keep good that unanimous oath?

There is some difference of opinion whether this clause should be enforced by national or by State authority; but surely that difference is not a very material one. If the slave is to be surrendered, it can be of but little consequence to him or to others by which authority it is done. And should any one in any case be content that his oath shall go unkept on a merely unsubstantial controversy as to how it shall be kept?

Again, in any law upon this subject, ought not all the safeguards of liberty known in civilized and humane jurisprudence to be introduced, so that a free man be not in any case, surrendered as a slave? And might it not be well at the same time to provide by law for the enforcement of that clause in the Constitution which guarantees that "the citizen of each State shall be entitled to all privileges and immunities of citizens in the several States"?

I take the official oath to-day with no mental reservations, and with no purpose to construe the Constitution or laws by any hypercritical rules. And while I do not choose now to specify particular acts of Congress as proper to be enforced, I do suggest that it will be much safer for all, both in official and private stations, to conform to and abide by all those acts which stand unrepealed, than to violate any of them, trusting to find impunity in having them held to be unconstitutional.

It is seventy-two years since the first inauguration of a President under our National Constitution. During that period, fifteen different and greatly distinguished citizens have, in succession, administered the executive branch of the government. They have conducted it through many perils, and generally with great success. Yet with all this scope of precedent, I now enter upon the same task for the brief constitutional term of four years under great and peculiar difficulty. A disruption of the Federal Union, heretofore only menaced, is now formidably attempted.

I hold that, in contemplation of universal law and of the Constitution, the union of these States is perpetual. Perpetuity is implied, if not expressed, in the fundamental law of all national governments. It is safe to assert that no government proper ever had a provision in its organic law for its own termination. Continue to execute all the express provisions of our National Constitution, and the Union will endure forever—it being impossible to destroy it except by some action not provided for in the instrument itself.

Again, if the United States be not a government proper, but an association of States in the nature of contract merely, can it, as a contract, be peaceably unmade by less than all the parties who made it? One party to a contract may violate it—break it, so as to speak; but does it not require all to lawfully rescind it?

Descending from these general principles, we find the proposition that in legal contemplation the Union is perpetual confirmed by the history of the Union itself. The Union is much older than the Constitution. It was formed, in fact, by the Articles of Association in 1774. It was matured and continued by the Declaration of Independence in 1776. It was further matured, and the faith of all the then thirteen states expressly plighted and engaged that it should be perpetual by the Articles of Confederation in 1778. And, finally, one of the declared objects for ordaining and establishing the Constitution was "to form a more perfect Union."

But if the destruction of the Union by one or by part of the States be lawfully possible, the Union is less perfect than before the Constitution, having lost the vital element of perpetuity.

It follows from these views that no State upon its own mere notion can lawfully get out of the Union; and resolves and ordinances to that effect are legally void; and that acts of violence, within any State or States, against the authority of the United States, are insurrectionary or revolutionary, according to circumstances.

I therefore consider that, in view of the Constitution and the laws, the Union is unbroken; and to the extent of my ability I shall take care, as the Constitution itself expressly enjoins upon me, that the laws of the Union be faithfully executed in all the States. Doing this I deem to be only a simple duty on my part; and I shall perform it so far as practicable, unless my rightful masters, the American people, shall withhold the requisite means, or in some authoritative manner direct the contrary. I trust this will not be regarded as a menace, but only as the declared purpose of the Union that it will constitutionally defend and maintain itself.

In doing this there need be no bloodshed or violence; and there shall be none, unless it be forced upon the national authority. The power confided to me will be used to hold, to occupy, and possess the property and places belonging to the government, and to collect the duties and imposts; but beyond what may be necessary for these objects, there will be no invasion, no using of force against or among the people anywhere. Where hostility to the United States, in any interior locality, shall be so great and universal as to prevent competent resident citizens from holding the Federal offices, there will be no attempt to force obnoxious strangers among the people for that object. While the strict legal right may exist in the government to enforce the exercise of these officers the attempt to do so would be so irritating, and so nearly impracticable, withal, that I deem it better to forego for the time such use of these offices.

The mails, unless repelled, will continue to be furnished in all parts of the Union. So far as possible, the people everywhere shall have that sense of perfect security which is most favorable to calm thought and reflection. The course here indicated will be followed unless current events and experience shall show a modification or change to be proper, and in every case and exigency my best discretion will be exercised according to circumstances actually existing, and with a view and a hope of peaceful solution of the national troubles and the restoration of fraternal sympathies and affections.

That there are persons in one section or another who seek to destroy the Union at all events, and are glad of any pretext to do it, I will neither affirm nor deny; but if there be such, I need address no word to them. To those, however, who really love the Union may I not speak?

Before entering upon so grave a matter as the destruction of our national fabric, with all its benefits, its memories, and its hopes, would it not be wise to ascertain precisely why we do it? Will you hazard so desperate a step while there is any possibility that any portion of the ills you fly from have no real existence? Will you, while the certain ills you fly to are greater than all the real ones you fly from——Will you risk the commission of so fearful a mistake?

Majority Opinion Is the Only True Sovereign

All profess to be content in the Union if all constitutional rights can be maintained. Is it true, then, that any right, plainly written in the Constitution, has been denied? I think not. Happily the human mind is so constituted that no party can reach to the audacity of doing this. Think, if you can, of a single instance in which a plainly written provision of the Constitution has ever been denied. If, by the mere force of numbers, a majority should deprive a minority of any clearly written constitutional right, it might, in a moral point of view, justify revolution—certainly would if such a right were a vital one. But such is not our case. All the vital rights of minorities and of individuals are so plainly assured to them by affirmations and negations, guarantees and prohibitions, in the Constitution, that controversies never arise concerning them. But no organic law can ever be framed with a provision specifically applicable to every question which may occur in practical administration. No foresight can anticipate, nor any document of reasonable length contain, express provisions for all possible questions. Shall fugitives from labor be surrendered by national or by state authority? The Constitution does not expressly say. *May* Congress prohibit slavery in the Territories? The Constitution does not expressly say. *Must* Congress protect slavery in the Territories? The Constitution does not expressly say.

From questions of this class spring all our constitutional controversies, and we divide upon them into majorities and minorities. If the minority will not acquiesce, the majority must, or the government must cease. There is no other alternative; for continuing the government is acquiescence on one side or the other.

If a minority in such case will secede rather than acquiesce, they make a precedent which in turn will divide and ruin them; for a minority of their own will secede from them whenever a majority refuses to be controlled by such a minority. For instance, why may not any portion of a new confederacy a year or two hence arbitrarily secede again, precisely as portions of the present Union now claim to secede from it? All who cherish disunion sentiments are now being educated to the exact temper of doing this.

Is there such perfect identity of interests among the States to compose a new Union, as to produce harmony only, and prevent renewed secession?

Plainly, the central idea of secession is the essence of anarchy. A majority held in restraint by constitutional checks and limitations, and always changing easily with deliberate changes of popular opinions and sentiments, is the only true sovereign of a free people. Whoever rejects it does, of necessity, fly to anarchy or to despotism. Unanimity is impossible; the rule of a minority, as a permanent arrangement, is wholly inadmissible; so that rejecting the majority principle, anarchy or despotism in some form is all that is left.

I do not forget the position assumed by some, that constitutional questions are to be decided by the Supreme Court; nor do I deny that such decisions must be binding, in any case, upon the parties to a suit, as to the object of that suit, while they are also entitled to very high respect and consideration in all parallel cases by all other departments of the government. And while it is obviously possible that such decision may be erroneous in any given case, still the evil effect following it, being limited to that particular case, with the chance that it may be over-ruled and never become a precedent for other cases, can better be borne than could the evils of a different practice. At the same time, the candid citizen must confess that if the policy of the government, upon vital questions affecting the whole people, is to be irrevocably fixed by decisions of the Supreme Court, the instant they are made, in ordinary litigation between parties in personal actions, the people will have ceased to be their own rulers, having to that extent practically resigned their government into the hands of that eminent tribunal. Nor is there in this view any assault upon the court or the judges. It is a duty from which they may not shrink to decide cases properly brought before them, and it is no fault of theirs if others seek to turn their decisions to political purposes.

One section of our country believes slavery is right, and ought to be extended, while the others believe it is wrong, and ought not to be extended. This is the only substantial dispute. The fugitive-slave clause of the Constitution, and the law of the suppression of the foreign slave-trade, are each as well enforced, perhaps as any law can ever be in a community where the moral sense of the people imperfectly supports the law itself. The great body of the people abide by the dry legal obligation in both cases and a few break over in each. This, I think, cannot be perfectly cured; and it would be worse in both cases, after the separation of the sections than before. The foreign slave-trade, now imperfectly suppressed, would be ultimately revived, without restriction, in one section, while fugitive slaves, now only partially surrendered, would not be surrendered at all by the other.

Physically speaking, we cannot separate. We cannot remove our respective sections from each other, nor build an impassable wall between them. A husband and wife may be divorced, and go out of the presence and beyond the reach of each other; but the different parts of our country cannot do this. They cannot but remain face to face, and intercourse, either amicable or hostile, must continue between them. Is it possible then to make that intercourse more advantageous or more satisfactory after separation than before? Can aliens make treaties easier than friends can make laws? Can treaties be more faithfully enforced between aliens than laws can among friends? Suppose you go to war, you cannot fight always; and when, after much loss on both sides, and no gain on either, you cease fighting, the identical old questions of intercourse are again upon you.

This country, with its institutions, belongs to the people who inhabit it. Whenever they shall grow weary of the existing government, they can exercise their constitutional right of amending it, or their revolutionary right to dismember or overthrow it. I cannot be ignorant of the fact that many worthy and patriotic citizens are desirous of having the National Constitution amended. While I make no recommendation of amendments, I fully recognize the rightful authority of the people over the whole subject, to be exercised in either of the modes prescribed in the instrument itself; and I should, under existing circumstances, favor rather than oppose, a fair opportunity being afforded the people to act upon it. I will venture to add that to me the convention mode seems preferable, in that it allows amendments to originate with the people themselves, instead of only permitting them to take or reject propositions originated by others not specially chosen for the purpose, and which might not be precisely such as they would wish to either accept or refuse. I understand a proposed amendment to the Constitution—which amendment, however, I have not seen—has passed Congress, to the effect that the Federal Government shall never interfere with the domestic institutions of the States, including that of persons held to service. To avoid misconstruction of what I have said, I depart from my purpose not to speak of particular amendments so far as to say that, holding such a provision to now be implied constitutional law, I have no objection to its being made express and irrevocable.

The chief magistrate derives all his authority from the people, and they have conferred none upon him to fix terms for the separation of the States. The people themselves can do this also if they choose; but the executive, as such, has nothing to do with it. His duty is to administer the present government, as it came to his hands, and to transmit it, unimpaired by him, to his successor.

Why should there not be a patient confidence in the ultimate justice of the people? Is there any better or equal hope in the world? In our present differences is either party without faith of being in the right? If the Almighty Ruler of Nations, with His eternal truth and justice, be on your side of the North, or on yours of the South, that truth and that justice will surely prevail by the judgment of this great tribunal of the American people.

By the frame of the government under which we live, this same people have wisely given their public servants but little power for mischief; and have, with equal wisdom, provided for the return of that little to their own hands at very short intervals. While the people retain their virtue and vigilance, no administration, by any extreme of wickedness or folly, can very seriously injure the government in the short space of four years.

My countrymen, one and all, think calmly and well upon this whole subject. Nothing valuable can be lost by taking time. If there be an object to hurry any one of you in hot haste to a step which you would never take deliberately, that object will be frustrated by taking time; but no good object can be frustrated by it. Such of you as are now dissatisfied, still have the old Constitution unimpaired, and, on the sensitive point, the laws of your own framing under it; while the new administration will have no immediate power, if it would, to change either. If it were admitted that you who are dissatisfied hold the right side in dispute, there still is no good reason for precipitate action. Intelligence, patriotism, Christianity, and a firm reliance on Him who has never yet forsaken this favored land, are still competent to adjust in the best way all our present difficulties.

In your hands, my dissatisfied countrymen, and not in mine, is the momentous issue of civil war. The government will not assail you. You can have no conflict without being yourselves the aggressors. You have no oath registered in heaven to destroy the government, while I shall have the most solemn one to "preserve, protect and defend" it.

I am loath to close. We are not enemies, but friends. We must not be enemies. Though passion may have strained it, it must not break our bond of affection. The mystic chords of memory, stretching from every battlefield and patriot grave to every living heart and hearthstone all over this broad land, will yet swell the chorus of the Union when again touched, as surely they will be, by the better angels of our nature.

GREATEST SPEECH IN AMERICAN HISTORY

Speech Delivered by Abraham Lincoln at Gettysburg, on November 19, 1863, Four Months After the Greatest Battle on American Soil. Greatest Address in Magnanimity of Spirit, Simplicity, Brevity, and Historical Import in American Annals

OURSCORE and seven years ago our fathers brought forth on this continent a new nation, conceived in liberty, and dedicated to the proposition that all men are created equal.

Now we are engaged in a great civil war, testing whether that nation, or any nation, so conceived and so dedicated, can long endure. We are met on a great battle-field of that war. We have come to dedicate a portion of that field as a final resting place for those who here gave their lives that that nation might live. It is altogether fitting and proper that we should do this.

But, in a larger sense, we cannot dedicate—we cannot consecrate—we cannot hallow—this ground. The brave men, living and dead, who struggled here, have consecrated it far above our poor power to add or detract. The world will little note nor long remember what we say here, but it can never forget what they did here. It is for us, the living, rather, to be dedicated here to the unfinished work which they who fought here have thus far so nobly advanced. It is rather for us to be here dedicated to the great task remaining before us—that from these honored dead we take increased devotion to that cause for which they gave the last full measure of devotion; that we here highly resolve that these dead shall not have died in vain; that this nation, under God, shall have a new birth of freedom; and that government of the people, by the people, for the people, shall not perish from the earth.

Magnificent Tribute to American Character in Which Lincoln at the Close of the Greatest War of Brother Against Brother that the World Had Ever Known Appealed for Love and Brotherhood at His Second Inauguration, March 4, 1865

FELLOW-COUNTRYMEN: At this second appearing to take the oath of the presidential office, there is less occasion for an extended address than there was at the first. Then a statement, somewhat in detail, of a course to be pursued, seemed fitting and proper. Now, at the expiration of four years, during which public declarations have been constantly called forth on every point and phase of the great contest which still absorbs the attention and engrosses the energies of the nation, little that is new could be presented. The progress of our arms, upon which all else chiefly depends, is as well known to the public as to myself; and it is, I trust, reasonably satisfactory and encouraging to all. With high hope for the future, no prediction in regard to it is ventured.

On the occasion corresponding to this four years ago, all thoughts were anxiously directed to an impending civil war. All dreaded it—all sought to avert it. While the inaugural address was being delivered from this place, devoted altogether to saving the Union without war, insurgent agents were in the city seeking to destroy it without war—seeking to dissolve the Union, and divide effects, by negotiation. Both parties deprecated war; but one of them would make war rather than let the nation survive; and the other would rather accept war than let it perish. And the war came.

With Malice Toward None—With Charity for All

One-eighth of the whole population were colored slaves, not distributed generally over the Union, but localized in the southern part of it. These slaves constituted a peculiar and powerful interest. All knew that this interest was, somehow, the cause of the war. To strengthen, perpetuate, and extend this interest was the object for which the insurgents would rend the Union, even by war; while the government claimed no right to do more than restrict the territorial enlargement of it.

Neither party expected for the war the magnitude or the duration which it has already attained. Neither anticipated that the cause of the conflict might cease with, or even before, the conflict itself should cease. Each looked for an easier triumph, and a result less fundamental and astounding. Both read the same Bible, and pray to the same God; and each invokes His aid against the other. It may seem strange that any men should dare to ask a just God's assistance in wringing their bread from the sweat of other men's faces; but let us judge not, that we be not judged. The prayers of both could not be answered—that of neither has been answered fully.

The Almighty has His own purposes. "Woe unto the world because of offenses! For it must needs be that offenses come; but woe to that man by whom the offense cometh." If we shall suppose that American slavery is one of those offenses which, in the providence of God, must needs come, but which, having continued through His appointed time, He now wills to remove, and that He gives to both North and South this terrible war, as the woe due to those by whom the offense came, shall we discern therein any departure from those divine attributes which the believers in a living God always ascribe to Him? Fondly do we hope—fervently do we pray—that this mighty scourge of war may speedily pass away. Yet, if God wills that it continue until all the wealth piled by the bondman's two hundred and fifty years of unrequited toil shall be sunk, and until every drop of blood drawn with the lash shall be paid by another drawn with the sword, as was said three thousand years ago, so still it must be said, "The judgments of the Lord are true and righteous altogether."

With malice toward none; with charity for all; with firmness in the right, as God gives us to see the right, let us strive on to finish the work we are in; to bind up the nation's wounds; to care for him whom shall have borne the battle, and for his widow, and his orphan—to do all which may achieve and cherish a just and lasting peace among ourselves, and with all nations.

"Work, work, work!"

"Hold on with a bull-dog grip."

"It's all in that one word, *Thorough*."

"Freedom is the last, best hope of earth."

"Nothing valuable can be lost by taking time."

"Calling a sheep's tail a leg doesn't make it so."

"Wealth is a superfluity of what we don't need."

"Many have got into a *habit* of being dissatisfied."

"Disenthrall ourselves, then we shall save ourselves."

"When you can't remove an obstacle, *plough around it !*"

"Discourage litigation. There will still be business enough."

"God bless my mother! All I am or hope to be I owe to her."

LAST PUBLIC SPEECH OF ABRAHAM LINCOLN

Speech Delivered by Lincoln on April 11, 1865, Three Days Before His Assassination in Which He Appeals to the American People to Join Hands in Peace and Build a Re-United Nation to Stand Forever as a Beacon of Liberty to the People of the Earth

WE meet this evening not in sorrow, but in gladness of heart. The evacuation of Petersburg and Richmond, and the surrender of the principal insurgent army, give hope of a righteous and speedy peace, whose joyous expression cannot be restrained. In the midst of this, however, He from whom all blessings flow must not be forgotten. A call for a national thanksgiving is being prepared, and will be duly promulgated. Nor must those whose harder part give us the cause of rejoicing be overlooked. Their honors must not be parceled out with others. I myself was near the front, and had the high pleasure of transmitting much of the good news to you; but no part of the honor for plan or execution is mine. To General Grant, his skillful officers and brave men, all belongs. The gallant navy stood ready, but was not in reach to take active part.

By these recent successes, the reinauguration of the national authority—reconstruction—which has had a large share of thought from the first is pressed much more closely upon our attention. It is fraught with great difficulty. Unlike a case of war between independent nations, there is no authorized organ for us to treat with—no one man has authority to give up the rebellion for any other man. We simply must begin with and mold from disorganized and discordant elements. Nor is it a small additional embarrassment that we, the loyal people, differ among ourselves as to the mode, manner, and measure of reconstruction. As a general rule, I abstain from reading the reports of attacks upon myself, wishing not to be provoked by that to which I cannot properly offer an answer. In spite of this precaution, however, it comes to my knowledge that I am much censured for some supposed agency in setting up and seeking to sustain the new State government of Louisiana.

In this I have done just so much and no more than the public knows. In the annual message of December, 1863, and in the accompanying proclamation, I presented a plan of reconstruction, as the phrase goes, which I promised, if adopted by any State, should be acceptable to and sustained by the executive government of the nation. I distinctly stated that this was not the only plan which might possibly be acceptable, and I also distinctly protested that the executive claimed no right to say when or whether members should be admitted to seats in Congress from such States. This plan was in advance submitted to the then Cabinet, and distinctly approved by every member of it. One of them suggested that I should then and in that connection apply the Emancipation Proclamation to the theretofore excepted parts of Virginia and Louisiana; that I should drop the suggestion about apprenticeship for freed people, and that I should omit the protest against my own power in regard to the admission of members to Congress. But even he approved every part and parcel of the plan which has since been employed or touched by the action of Louisiana.

The new constitution of Louisiana, declaring emancipation for the whole State, practically applies the proclamation to the part previously excepted. It does not adopt apprenticeship for freed people, and it is silent, as it could not well be otherwise, about the admission of members to Congress. So that, as it applies to Louisiana, every member of the Cabinet fully approved the plan. The message went to Congress, and I received many commendations of the plan, written and verbal, and not a single objection to it from any professed emancipationist came to my knowledge until after the news reached Washington that the people of Louisiana had begun to move in accordance with it. From about July, 1862, I had corresponded with different persons supposed to be interested in seeking a reconstruction of a State government for Louisiana. When the message of 1863, with the plan before mentioned, reached New Orleans, General Banks wrote me that he was confident that the people, with his military co-operation, would reconstruct substantially on that plan. I wrote to him and some of them to try it. They tried it, and the result is known. Such has been my only agency in getting up the Louisiana government.

As to sustaining it, my promise is out, as before stated. But as bad promises are better broken than kept, I shall treat this as a bad promise, and break it whenever I shall be convinced that keeping it is adverse to the public interest; but I have not yet been so convinced. I have been shown a letter on this subject, supposed to be an able one, in which the writer expresses regret that my mind has not seemed to be definitely fixed on the question whether the seceded States, so called, are in the Union or out of it. It would perhaps add astonishment to his regret were he to learn that since I have found professed Union men endeavoring to make that question, I have purposely forborne any public expression upon it. As appears to me, that question has not been, nor yet is, a practically material one, and that any discussion of it, while it thus remains practically immaterial, could have no effect other than the mischievous one of dividing our friends. As yet, whatever it may hereafter become, that question is bad as the basis of a controversy and good for nothing at all—a merely pernicious abstraction.

We all agree that the seceded States, so called, are out of their proper, practical relation with the Union, and that the sole object of the government, civil and military, in regard to those States, is to again get them into that proper practical relation. I believe that it is not only possible, but in fact easier, to do this without deciding or even considering whether these States have ever been out of the Union, than with it. Finding themselves safely at home, it would be utterly immaterial whether they had ever been abroad. Let us all join in doing the acts necessary to restoring the proper practical relations between these States and the Union, and each forever after innocently indulge his own opinion whether in doing the acts he brought the States from without into the Union, or only gave them proper assistance, they never having been out of it. The amount of constituency, so to speak, on which the new Louisiana government rests, would be more satisfactory to all if it contained 50,000 or 30,000, or even 20,000, instead of only about 12,000, as it does. It is also unsatisfactory to some that the elective franchise is not given to the colored man. I would myself prefer that it were now conferred on the very intelligent, and on those who serve our cause as soldiers.

Still, the question is not whether the Louisiana government, as it stands, is quite all that is desirable. The question is, will it be wiser to take it as it is and help to improve it, or to reject and disperse it? Can Louisiana be brought into proper practical relation with the Union sooner by sustaining or by discarding her new State government? Some twelve thousand voters in the heretofore slave State of Louisiana have sworn allegiance to the Union, assumed to be the rightful political power of the State, held elections, organized a State government, adopted a free-State constitution, giving the benefit of public schools equally to black and white, and empowering the legislature to confer the elective franchise upon the colored man. Their legislature has already voted to ratify the constitutional amendment recently passed by Congress, abolishing slavery throughout the nation. These 12,000 persons are thus fully committed to the Union and to perpetual freedom in the State—committed to the very things, and nearly all the things, the nation wants—and they ask the nation's recognition and its assistance to make good their committal.

Now, if we reject and spurn them, we do our utmost to disorganize and disperse them. We, in effect, say to the white man: You are worthless or worse; we will neither help you, nor be helped by you. To the blacks we say: This cup of liberty which these, your old masters, hold to your lips we will dash from you, and leave you to the chances of gathering the spilled and scattered contents in some vague and undefined when, where, and how. If this course, discouraging and paralyzing both white and black, has any tendency to bring Louisiana into proper practical relations with the Union, I have so far been unable to perceive it. If, on the contrary, we recognize and sustain the new government of Louisiana, the converse of all this is made true. We encourage the hearts and nerve the arms of the 12,000 to adhere to their work, and argue for it, and proselyte for it, and fight for it, and feed it, and grow it, and ripen it to a complete success. The colored man, too, in seeing all united for him, is inspired with vigilance, and energy, and daring, to the same end. Grant that he desires the elective franchise, will he not attain it sooner by saving the already advanced steps toward it than by running backward over them? Concede that the new government of Louisiana is only what it should be, as the egg is to the fowl, we shall sooner have the fowl by hatching the egg than by smashing it.

Again, if we reject Louisiana, we also reject one vote in favor of the proposed amendment to the national Constitution. To meet this proposition, it has been argued that no more than three-fourths of those States which have not attempted secession are necessary to validly ratify the amendment. I do not commit myself against this further than to say that such a ratification would be questionable, and sure to be persistently questioned, while a ratification by three-fourths of all the States would be unquestioned and unquestionable. I repeat the question: Can Louisiana be brought into proper practical relation with the Union sooner by sustaining or by discarding her new State government? What has been said of Louisiana will apply generally to other States. And yet so great peculiarities pertain to each State, and such important and sudden changes occur in the same State, and withal so new and unprecedented is the whole case that no exclusive and inflexible plan can safely be prescribed as to details and collaterals. Such an exclusive and inflexible plan would surely become a new entanglement. Important principles may and must be inflexible. In the present situation, as the phrase goes, it may be my duty to make some new announcement to the people of the South. I am considering, and shall not fail to act when satisfied that action will be proper,

"I desire to see the time when education, by its means, morality, sobriety, enterprise, and integrity, shall become much more general than at present, and should be gratified to have it in my power to contribute something to the advancement of any measure which might have a tendency to accelerate the happy period."

"And when the victory shall be complete,—when there shall be neither a slave nor a drunkard on earth,—how proud the title of that land, which may truly claim to be the birthplace and the cradle of both those resolutions that shall have ended in that victory! How nobly distinguished that people, who shall have planted, and nurtured to maturity, both the political and moral freedom of their species!"

"Capital has its rights, which are as worthy of protection as any rights nor is it denied that there is, and probably always will be, a relation between labor and capital, producing mutual benefits . . . No men living are more worthy to be trusted than those who toil up from poverty—none less inclined to take or touch aught which they have not honestly earned."

"In regard to the Great Book, I have only to say that it is the best gift which God has given man. All the good from the Saviour of the world is communicated to us through this Book. But for this Book we could not know right from wrong. All those things to man are contained in it."

"Give the Boys a chance." "We cannot escape history." "I can bear censure, but not insult!" "Don't swap horses in crossing a stream." "Let us have faith that right makes might." "Public opinion in this country is everything." "I know I am right because I know Liberty is right." "Is a man to blame for having a pair of cowardly legs?"

"That some are rich shows that others may become rich."

"Come what will, I will keep my faith with friend and foe."

"Faith in God is indispensable to successful statesmanship."

"There is no grievance that is a fit object of redress by mob law."

"My boy, never *try* to be President! If you do, you never will be."

"The dogmas of the quiet past are inadequate to the stormy present."

"The Lord must love the common people—that's why he made so many of them."

"Keep that (temperance) pledge and it will be the best act of your life."

"No man is good enough to govern another man without that other man's consent."

"Familiarize yourself with the chains of bondage and you prepare your own limbs to wear them."

"A man has no time to spend in quarrels. If any man ceases to attack me I never remember the past against him."

"The importance for man and beast of the prescribed weekly rest, the sacred rights of Christian soldiers and sailors, a becoming deference to the best sentiments of a Christian people, and a due regard for the divine will, demand that Sunday labor be reduced to the measure of strict necessity."

The Portrait Life of Lincoln

PART V

A Chronology of the Historic Events in the
Growth of the American Nation
from the Birth to the Death of Lincoln

Chronology of the Life of Lincoln—1809-1817

1809—February 12; Abraham Lincoln born at Hodgensville, Hardin County, Kentucky; parents, Thomas and Nancy Hanks Lincoln.

February 28; Embargo Act repealed.

March 1; Territory of Illinois organized.

March 4; James Madison inaugurated fourth President of the United States, succeeding Thomas Jefferson.

1810—February 12; Abraham Lincoln's first birthday; still living in log cabin where he was born.

March 23; Napoleon, in his conquest of the world, decrees that all American vessels entering French ports shall be seized and condemned.

June 1; Total population of the United States 7,239,822, of which 1,191,363 are colored slaves.

1811—January 9; Entire militia of New Orleans is called out to suppress negro insurrection.

February 12; Abraham Lincoln's second birthday; still living in log cabin where he was born.

October 11; First steam ferry-boat in the world across the Hudson river at New York.

October 29; First steamboat on western waters leaves Pittsburg for New Orleans.

November 7; Battle of Tippecanoe, in warfare with Indians.

November 9; Henry Clay, age 34, Speaker of House of Representatives, having served two terms in United States Senate.

1812—January 9; Society is formed at Trenton for organizing a colony of colored people.

February 12; Abraham Lincoln's third birthday; still living at cabin where he was born.

March 9; President Madison reveals to Congress a plot to destroy the Union.

April 30; Louisiana admitted into the Union.

June 4; Territory of Missouri established.

June 18; Congress declared war against England; the naval victories of the Americans over the greatest of naval powers aroused intense excitement.

June 18; New England threatens secession from the Union (the first in United States history) while repudiating war with England.

June 23; First naval encounter in War of 1812.

July 12; First land engagements. Hull invades Canada.

August 16; Surrender of Detroit to British.

August 19; *Constitution* destroys British ship-of-war, *Guerriere,* off Banks of Newfoundland.

October 13; Americans attack Queenstown Heights, in Canada, and are severely repulsed.

October 13; *Wasp* victorious over the British ship, *Frolic,* off the coast of North Carolina.

November 1; Daniel Webster enters political life; age 30.

1813—February 12; Abraham Lincoln's fourth birthday; moved during this year from cabin in which he was born to Knob Creek, fifteen miles distant, where he met the first soldier he had ever seen, during War of 1812 which was now raging.

1813—March 4; Inauguration of James Madison into his second term as President of the United States.

March 20; Great Britain proclaims Atlantic coast of America under blockade.

April 23; Birth of Stephen A. Douglas at Brendon, in Vermont, who was to become Lincoln's greatest political rival.

May 10; First ferry connects Brooklyn with New York.

June 1; *Chesapeake* captured by the British ship, *Shannon.* Captain Lawrence fatally wounded.

1814—January 14; Daniel Webster's first speech in the House on the Enlistment Bill; age 32.

February 12; Abraham Lincoln's fifth birthday; he begins his first schooling.

August 24; City of Washington captured by the British; President and Cabinet flee; National Capitol burned.

September 13; National hymn, "The Star Spangled Banner," composed during bombardment of Fort McHenry near Baltimore.

December 15; Hartford Convention with object of secession. Peace between England and United States ended session. Federalist party ruined.

December 19; Birth of Edwin B. Stanton at Steubenville, Ohio, who was to become Lincoln's great secretary of war.

December 24; Peace between England and America negotiated through Treaty of Ghent.

1815—January 8; American victory at battle of New Orleans, under Andrew Jackson.

June 30; Americans dictate terms of peace at Algiers.

February 12; Abraham Lincoln's sixth birthday; during this year he barely escaped drowning in Knob Creek.

March 3; United States declares war against Algiers.

June 18; Hostilities cease between the United States and England; estimated cost of war, $85,500,000.

August 1; First Peace Society in the world is founded.

1816—February 12; Abraham Lincoln's seventh birthday; removed this year with his parents to Gentryville, Spencer County, Indiana, crossing the Ohio river from Kentucky on a raft.

December 11; Indiana admitted into the Union.

1817—February 12; Abraham Lincoln's eighth birthday; living in open camp in Indiana wilderness; wielding the ax in the primeval forest.

March 4; James Monroe of Virginia, inaugurated fifth President of the United States.

July 4; Construction of the Erie Canal begins.

August 2; First steamship arrives at St. Louis.

November 20; Outbreak of Seminole Indian War.

December 10; Mississippi admitted into the Union.

December 28; American Colonization Society organized at Washington to return negroes to Africa.

1818—February 12; Abraham Lincoln's ninth birthday; living in rough cabin of unhewn timbers in Indiana, which he helped his father to build.

April 4; Act establishing flag of the United States, with thirteen horizontal stripes, alternating red and white, and a white star in a blue field for each state.

August 23; First steamboat trip on Lake Erie.

October 5; Death of Nancy Hanks, Lincoln's mother, at Pigeon Creek, Indiana; age 35.

December 3; Illinois admitted to the Union.

December 18; Great agitation of Slavery Question by petition of Missouri for admission to Union as a slave state.

1819—February 12; Abraham Lincoln's tenth birthday; living with his father and sister Sarah (Nancy) in Indiana wilderness.

February 17; Bill presented to Congress for the gradual emancipation of the slaves in Missouri; fails to pass Senate.

February 22; Treaty with Spain in which the United States gains possession of Florida and surrenders all claim to Texas.

May 26; First steamship crosses the Atlantic, "The Savannah."

October 24; Erie Canal is open from Utica to Rome.

December 1; First national financial crisis occurs; many banks barely escape insolvency; national debt $95,529,648.

December 2; Second marriage of Abraham Lincoln's father, Thomas Lincoln, to Sarah Rush Johnston, at Elizabethtown, Kentucky.

December 14; Alabama admitted to the Union.

1820—February 12; Abraham Lincoln's eleventh birthday; walking nine miles a day to and from the frontier school.

March 2; Missouri Compromise temporarily quells anti-slavery agitation.

March 3; Maine admitted into the Union.

May 5; Congress recognizes slave trade to be piracy and prohibits citizens from engaging in it under penalty of death; total slaves 2,009,031. Webster and Calhoun denounce agitators against the slave system.

June 1; First steamship line between New York and New Orleans.

1821—February 12; Abraham Lincoln's twelfth birthday; he was now under the influence of his stepmother, who had awakened in him an eagerness for learning.

March 4; James Monroe of Virginia, inaugurated into his second term as President of the United States.

August 1; Liberia is secured for the negro colonization by the American Colonization Society.

August 10; Missouri admitted into the Union amid a tempest of political excitement; anti-slavery agitation becomes violent.

August 10; City Council of Charleston, South Carolina, prohibits opening of night or Sunday school for the instruction of negro slaves.

1822—February 1; First cotton mill is erected in Massachusetts.

1822—February 12; Abraham Lincoln's thirteenth birthday; he was now working on the farm and acting as chore boy for the neighbors, devoting his leisure to ciphering on a wooden shovel and on the logs of his cabin.

April 27; Birth of Ulysses S. Grant at Point Pleasant, Ohio, who was to bring victory to Lincoln as commander of the armies in the Civil War.

1823—February 1; Stephen F. Austin obtains from Mexico a grant of land in Texas for colonization.

February 12; Abraham Lincoln's fourteenth birthday; attending Andrew Crawford's neighborhood school, where he wrote his first essay against cruelty to animals.

June 1; First steam power printing press in New York.

December 2; Declaration of the Monroe Doctrine: a protest against interference of any European power on the American continent.

1824—February 12; Abraham Lincoln's fifteenth birthday; it was about this time that he began to read eagerly, and is said to have borrowed all the books within fifty miles of his home.

May 22; Protective tariff bill adopted; opposed by the South and New England.

August 10; Robert Owen of Scotland establishes a Communistic settlement in Indiana.

August 15; Lafayette revisits America.

1825—February 12; Abraham Lincoln's sixteenth birthday; employed in Indiana as ferryman and butcher at six dollars per month.

March 4; John Quincy Adams inaugurated sixth President of the United States.

October 1; Working people begin to discuss question of shorter hours and greater safety.

October 26—Erie Canal completed, 363 miles long; cost $7,500,000; connects Great Lakes with seaboard at New York.

1826—February 12; Abraham Lincoln's seventeenth birthday; he now began to read his first law book and wrote a paper on the American Government.

July 4; Fiftieth anniversary of American Independence.

July 4; Death of John Adams, second president, and Thomas Jefferson, the third.

October 1; Morgan Anti-Mason excitement in politics.

October 7; First railroad in the United States, three miles long, at Quincy, Massachusetts.

October 10; Kerosene first used for illuminating purposes.

December 3; Birth of George B. McClellan at Philadelphia, Pennsylvania, who was to become Lincoln's first general in the Civil War.

1827—February 12; Abraham Lincoln's eighteenth birthday; during this year he earned his first dollar.

July 30; Protectionists hold a convention and demand higher tariff.

July —; Death of Lincoln's sister, Sarah (Nancy), age twenty.

1828—February 12; Abraham Lincoln's nineteenth birthday; he was now a giant youth of six feet, four inches; went on his first trip as a flat-boatsman down the Mississippi to New Orleans, at eight dollars a month.

May 15; First American dictionary of English language, by Noah Webster.

May 19; High protective tariff enacted, causing serious distress between the North and the South.

December 1; Political party known as Workingman's Association appears in principal cities.

December —; First steamboat in Boston Harbor.

1829—February 12; Abraham Lincoln's twentieth birthday; working as wood chopper, known as a backwoods orator, arguing on slavery and political subjects.

March 4; Andrew Jackson inaugurated seventh President of the United States; beginning of the Spoils System in American politics.

June 30; Robert E. Lee of Virginia, twenty-two years old; graduates at West Point.

August 8; First locomotive in the United States.

September 21; First public school in Baltimore.

September —; First asylum in the United States for the blind, at Boston.

——————— William Lloyd Garrison advocates immediate emancipation of the slaves.

——————— First emancipation of slaves on American Continent when Mexico issued a proclamation of emancipation.

1830—February 12; Abraham Lincoln's twenty-first birthday; preparing to leave Indiana with family for Illinois.

April 6; First settlement of Mormons, in Manchester, New York.

August 12; The first American railroad is completed; it connects Albany and Schenectady.

October 5; American ports are re-opened to British commerce.

1831—February 12; Abraham Lincoln's twenty-second birthday; helps his father build their new home in Illinois; works as a flat-boatsman, later acting as clerk in store at New Salem, Illinois.

April 21; Beginning of the Black Hawk War in Indiana.

April 26; Imprisonment for debt is abolished in New York.

August 21; Negro insurrection in Virginia, fifty whites killed.

1832—January 6; Founding of American Anti-Slavery Society by William Lloyd Garrison.

February 12; Abraham Lincoln's twenty-third birthday; volunteers in the Black Hawk War, and is chosen captain of his company; entered partnership in a store-keeping project, which soon failed; reads a copy of Blackstone's Commentaries on the Common Law.

May 21; First Democratic (so-called) National Convention meets in Baltimore.

1832—July 13; Henry R. Schoolcraft discovers the source of the Mississippi River.

August —; Abraham Lincoln defeated for state Legislature in Illinois.

November 1; First street railroad in the United States is opened between the City Hall and 14th Street, New York.

December 11; Nullification Proclamation issued by President Jackson.

December 31; Immigrants and other aliens rush to America—60,482 in fifteen months.

December —; "My Country, 'tis of Thee" is written by Samuel Francis Smith, New Center, Massachusetts.

December —; First house in Iowa is erected near Davenport.

1833—February 12; Abraham Lincoln's twenty-fourth birthday; burdened with debt, studies and practices surveying.

March 2; Bloody Bill passed by Congress to enforce tariff of 1832 which was declared null and void by South Carolina.

March 4; Andrew Jackson inaugurated into his second term as President of the United States.

March —; Texas begins a war against Mexico for independence.

March —; Anti-slavery societies formed in several states.

May 7; Abraham Lincoln appointed postmaster at New Salem, Illinois.

1834—February 12; Abraham Lincoln's twenty-fifth birthday; elected to the Legislature; meets Stephen A. Douglas; appointed second place on the Committee of Public Accounts and Expenditures by Speaker Hon. James Semple.

February 17; Treaty with Spain signed.

June 21; Invention of the reaping machine patented by Cyrus H. McCormick, of Virginia, which became the foundation of the great agricultural wealth of America.

June 30; Indian Territory is set apart exclusively for Indians.

November —; Abraham Lincoln elected to the state Legislature of Illinois.

1835—January 30; Attempted assassination of President Jackson.

February 10; Philadelphia is first lighted with gas .

February 12; Abraham Lincoln's twenty-sixth birthday; borrows money to be suitably clothed before going to the state capitol as a legislator; favors woman's suffrage, and raises his voice against slavery.

December 16; Great conflagration in New York City with a loss of $20,000,000.

December 23; Beginning of the Florida Indian War.

1836—January 11; A petition is presented to Congress praying that the institution of slavery may be abolished in the District of Columbia.

February 12; Abraham Lincoln's twenty-seventh birthday; licensed to practice law.

March 2; Texas declares her independence.

April —; Abraham Lincoln commences the practice of law in Springfield, Illinois.

May 14; Mexico acknowledges independence of Texas.

June 15; Arkansas admitted to the Union as the twenty-fifth state.

Chronology of the Life of Lincoln—1836-1845

1836—November —; Abraham Lincoln is re-elected to the Legislature of Illinois.

November —; Territory of Wisconsin organized.

1837—January 26; Congress admits Michigan into the Union as the twenty-sixth state.

February 12; Abraham Lincoln's twenty-eighth birthday; retired from postmastership at New Salem, Illinois.

March 3; Texas recognized as independent by United States, England and France.

March 4; Martin Van Buren of New York is inaugurated the eighth President of the United States.

March —; Abraham Lincoln protests against the pro-slavery action of the majority in the Legislature; entered on the journal of the Assembly.

May 5; The Creek Indian war begins.

December 1; The Cherokee Indian disturbance—caused by the enforced removal of the Indians to the West.

December 8; Wendell Phillips's first "abolition" speech in Faneuil Hall, Boston, to protest against the murder of Elijah P. Lovejoy.

December —; Samuel F. B. Morse first publicly exhibits his telegraph.

December 29; American sympathizers with Canadians in revolt against English rule attacked in Niagara River; known as "Patriot War."

1838—February 1; John Ericsson patents first screw-propeller.

February 12; Abraham Lincoln's twenty-ninth birthday; enters partnership in practice of law with John T. Stuart in Springfield, Illinois.

November —; Abraham Lincoln is re-elected to the state Legislature, and becomes leader of the Whigs.

November —; Abolitionists organize a political party in New York.

December 11; Congress; House passes a slavery "Gag-law."

December —; Government forcibly removes Cherokee Indians beyond the Mississippi.

1839—February 12; Abraham Lincoln's thirtieth birthday; during this year he is arguing against slavery, in the Legislature at Illinois.

June —; Governor of the territory of Florida offers a reward of two hundred dollars for every Indian killed or taken.

June —; Daguerreotypes first taken in the United States by Prof. J. W. Draper.

September 1; Ulysses S. Grant of Ohio enters the Military Academy at West Point; age seventeen.

1840—February 12; Abraham Lincoln's thirty-first birthday; during this year he is again re-elected to Legislature.

February —; Another pro-slavery "Gag-law" passes the House.

1841—February 12; Abraham Lincoln's thirty-second birthday; re-awakens interest in temperance; finds Stephen A. Douglas his rival in state legislature.

March 4; William Henry Harrison of Ohio is inaugurated ninth President of the United States, dies within a month (April 4) and John Tyler is inaugurated tenth President.

1841—September 4, 5; A riot against abolitionists and negroes occurs at Cincinnati.

October —; Uprising of slaves in Virginia.

October —; Elias Howe of Massachusetts, a mechanic, invents the first practical sewing machine.

1842—February 12; Abraham Lincoln's thirty-third birthday.

February 22; Abraham Lincoln addresses the Washingtonian Temperance Society at Springfield, favoring total abstinence and the temperance revolution.

March 30; First use of Anæsthetics in medical practice in America.

May 2; First governmental exploration of western country beyond the Missouri.

August 9; Lord Ashburton and Daniel Webster sign Treaty, establishing the Northwestern boundaries, and those extending westward along the Great Lakes; provides for the suppression of the African slave trade, and makes provision for the extradition of criminals.

September —; Duel between Abraham Lincoln and General Shields.

November 4; Abraham Lincoln marries Mary Todd of Lexington, Kentucky.

November —; Earliest actual finding of gold in California, in Los Angeles district.

November —; Anti-slavery meetings are broken up in many states; buildings damaged and its advocates assaulted.

1843—February 12; Abraham Lincoln's thirty-fourth birthday.

March 3; Congress appropriates $30,000 to aid Professor Morse in establishing the first telegraph line, between Washington and Baltimore.

June 30; Ulysses S. Grant graduates at West Point; he ranks number twenty-one in a class of thirty-nine.

June —; About 1,000 emigrants leave Westport on the Missouri frontier on a journey of 2,000 miles to Oregon and arrive in October.

August 1; Abraham Lincoln's son, Robert Todd Lincoln, born.

October 25; Fremont's expedition reaches the Columbia River in Oregon.

1844—February 12; Abraham Lincoln's thirty-fifth birthday.

February —; Both political parties in the North are divided by an anti-slavery and a pro-slavery wing.

February —; New England Workingmen's Association is organized in Boston.

1845—February 12; Abraham Lincoln's thirty-sixth birthday.

March 3; Florida (slave) admitted as the twenty-seventh state.

March 3; Congress reduces postage on letters to five cents within radius of three hundred miles; ten cents for greater distances.

March 4; James K. Polk, of Tennessee, is inaugurated the eleventh President.

December 29; Texas admitted as the twenty-eighth state; slavery is permitted.

December —; Order of United American Mechanics is founded.

1845—December —; Whigs oppose slavery. Southern Whigs, under lead of Henry Clay, now considered slavery an evil to be removed in some practical way, at some distant period, but not to be interfered with in the states where it existed.

1846—February 12; Abraham Lincoln's thirty-seventh birthday.

March 10; Abraham Lincoln's son, Edward Baker Lincoln, born—but died in infancy.

April 25; First engagement of the Mexican war at La Rosa.

May 8; American victory in battle of Palo Alto.

May 9; American victory in battle of Resaca de la Palma.

November —; Abraham Lincoln is elected to Congress from Illinois, a solitary Whig among seven Democrats.

December 28; Iowa (free) admitted into the Union as the twenty-ninth state.

1847—February 12; Abraham Lincoln's thirty-eighth birthday.

February 23; American victory in battle of Buena Vista.

February 23; American victory in battle of Sacramento.

July 26; First electric locomotive was exhibited and operated.

September 14; American army triumphantly enters city of Mexico.

December —; Abraham Lincoln and Andrew Jackson in the House of Representatives at Washington; Stephen A. Douglas and Jefferson Davis in the United States Senate.

December 22; Lincoln introduced his "spots" resolutions in Congress.

——— First use of postage stamps under governmental authority.

1848—February 12; Abraham Lincoln's thirty-ninth birthday; speaking in Massachusetts in the summer of this year against the Free Soil Party; introduced bill for the abolition of slavery in the District of Columbia late in the year; meets Seward for the first time.

February —; Discovery of gold hastens emigration to California.

May 29; Wisconsin (free) admitted to the Union as the thirtieth state.

July 4; Peace with Mexico is proclaimed.

July —; President Polk authorizes the United States Minister at Madrid to offer Spain $100,000,000 for Cuba; he obtains a curt refusal.

1849—February 12; Abraham Lincoln's fortieth birthday; studies and masters Euclid; seeks appointment as Commissioner of the General Land Office under President Taylor; fails to secure same; returns to law office in Springfield.

March 5; Zachary Taylor of Louisiana, inaugurated the twelfth President of the United States.

December —; Exciting debates occur in Congress on the Slavery Question; several Southern members threaten secession and Civil War if slavery is excluded from the territories.

December —; Gold dollars are first coined.

1850—February 12; Abraham Lincoln's forty-first birthday; declines lucrative offer to move to Chicago and enter partnership of leading law firm.

March 7; Daniel Webster delivers his memorable address against his anti-slavery friends, who regard it as a betrayal.

July 9; Death of President Taylor.

July 10; Vice-President Millard Fillmore of New York is inaugurated the thirteenth President of the United States.

July —; President Fillmore favors compromise measures with slavery.

September 9; New Mexico and Utah territories are organized.

September 9; California admitted into the Union as the thirty-first state; slavery excluded.

September 10; Congress passes the Fugitive Slave Bill.

September 20; Slave trade suppressed in District of Columbia to take effect January 1, 1851.

September 1; Total slaves in the United States, 3,204,313.

December 21; Abraham Lincoln's son, William Wallace Lincoln, born.

December —; Chicago organizes a Board of Trade; the city is lighted with gas.

1851—February 12; Abraham Lincoln's forty-second birthday; circuit lawyer.

February —; Death of Abraham Lincoln's father, Thomas Lincoln, age seventy-three years.

December 24; Fire consumes part of the National Capitol and the Congressional Library at Washington.

1852—February 12; Abraham Lincoln's forty-third birthday; joins the Sons of Temperance in Springfield.

June 29; Death of Henry Clay, age seventy-five.

August —; Lone Star Society is organized for the extension of National influence in the Western Hemisphere, and for the acquisition of Cuba and the Sandwich Islands.

October 24; Death of Daniel Webster, age seventy.

October —; "Uncle Tom's Cabin," by Mrs Harriet Beecher Stowe, causes sensation and inflames public mind against slavery.

1853—February 12; Abraham Lincoln's forty-fourth birthday.

March 4; Franklin Pierce of New Hampshire is inaugurated the fourteenth President of the United States.

April 4; Abraham Lincoln's son, Thomas Lincoln, born.

July 14; World's Fair; Crystal Palace opening at New York.

July —; "Know-Nothing" Society, a political organization, springs up—soon disappears.

July —; Washington Territory is organized.

December 30; Gadsden purchase consummated with Mexico securing additional territory for New Mexico and Arizona.

1854—January —; Slavery agitation is re-opened in Congress by Archibald Dixon of Kentucky (Democrat) who gives notice that the Missouri Compromise is to be repealed and new states will be given to slavery.

Chronology of the Life of Lincoln—1854-1861

1854—January —; Acrimonious debates on the extension of slavery engage the Senate for four months.

February 12; Abraham Lincoln's forty-fifth birthday.

March 31; Commodore Perry's treaty with Japan.

April 20; Massachusetts Emigrant Aid Company is organized with a fixed capital limited at $5,000,000.

May 30; President Pierce signs the Kansas-Nebraska Bill, which provides for the organization of the Kansas and Nebraska territories.

July —; Connecticut Legislature incorporates an Emigrant Aid Association.

October —; Abraham Lincoln challenges Stephen A. Douglas to a joint debate in the canvass for Congress.

1855—January —; First bridge across the Mississippi—completed at Minneapolis.

February 12; Abraham Lincoln's forty-sixth birthday.

February —; Anti-Slavery party becomes generally known as the Republican party; Whig party rapidly disappears.

February —; Struggle over the Slavery Question in Kansas.

1856—February 12; Abraham Lincoln's forty-seventh birthday; became Republican—and name was presented for Vice-President to the first National Convention.

May 22; Senator Sumner assaulted in Senate because of his anti-slavery speeches.

May 29; Lincoln delivers his famous "Lost Speech" at organization of Republican party at Bloomington, Illinois.

June 17; The Republican National Convention at Philadelphia denounces "those twin relics of barbarism, polygamy and slavery."

August 29; A band of pro-slavery men, under Captain Reid, defeats John Brown, the abolitionist of Osawatomie.

1857—February 12; Abraham Lincoln's forty-eighth birthday.

March 4; James Buchanan of Pennsylvania is inaugurated fifteenth President of the United States.

March 6; Dred Scott case confirms Northern feeling against slavery.

1858—February 12; Abraham Lincoln's forty-ninth birthday.

May —; Abraham Lincoln wins Armstrong murder trial as defending counsel.

May 11; Minnesota (free) admitted into the Union as the thirty-second state.

June 16; Lincoln delivers his celebrated opening speech in his campaign for the Senate at Springfield, Illinois.

August 5; Celebration of the successful laying of the Atlantic cable.

August 21; First of the famous Lincoln-Douglas debates at Ottawa, Illinois.

August 27; Second Lincoln-Douglas debate at Freeport, Illinois.

September 15; Third Lincoln-Douglas debate at Jonesboro, Illinois.

September 18; Fourth Lincoln-Douglas debate at Charleston, Illinois.

October 7; Fifth Lincoln-Douglas debate at Galesburg, Illinois.

1858—October 13; Sixth Lincoln-Douglas debate at Quincy, Illinois.

October 15; Seventh Lincoln-Douglas debate at Alton, Illinois.

1859—February 12; Abraham Lincoln's fiftieth birthday.

February 14; Oregon (free) admitted into the Union as the thirty-third state.

September —; Abraham Lincoln answers Douglas in Ohio.

October 16; John Brown makes a raid at Harper's Ferry, in Virginia, to free the slaves.

October —; Jefferson Davis addresses the Democratic State Convention of Mississippi in behalf of slavery and the extension of the slave territory.

December 2; John Brown hanged for treason at Charleston, West Virginia.

1860—February 12; Abraham Lincoln's fifty-first birthday.

February 27; Abraham Lincoln delivers his first great address in New York at Cooper Union.

May 18; Abraham Lincoln of Illinois nominated for President of the United States by the Republican party at Chicago; Hannibal Hamlin of Maine, Vice-President.

November 6; Abraham Lincoln elected President of the United States (Republican), receiving 1,866,452 votes; Stephen A. Douglas (Southern Democratic), 1,375,157; Breckinridge (Democratic), 845,763 Bell (Union), 589,581.

December 14; Senators and Representatives from eight Southern states issue addresses to their constituents, urging secession of separate states for the purpose of organizing a Southern Confederacy.

December 20; South Carolina secedes from the Union; this leads to Civil War between the North and the South.

December 26; Fort Sumter fortified by Major Anderson.

December 27-30; South Carolinians take possession of United States property in their state, except Fort Sumter.

December 31; There are thirty-three states in the Union; eighteen free and fifteen slave; this gives the control of the government to the free states.

1861—January 5; Steamship "Star of the West" sails with reinforcements and supplies for Major Anderson in charge of Fort Sumter.

January 9; First shot is fired in the Civil War, when the "Star of the West," approaching Fort Sumter, is attacked by the batteries of Fort Moultrie and compelled to retire.

January 9; Mississippi, the second state, secedes.

January 11; Florida, the third state, secedes.

January 11; Alabama, the fourth state, secedes.

January 19; Georgia, the fifth state, secedes.

January 26; Louisiana, the sixth state, secedes.

January 29; Kansas (free) is admitted into the Union as the thirty-fourth state.

February 1; Texas, the seventh state, secedes.

1861—February 4; Confederate Congress is organized in Alabama.

February 4; Peace Congress met at Washington.

February 4; Twenty-one states sent delegates to Washington in response to Virginia's call for peace conference to avert war. Conference failed.

February 11; Lincoln delivers farewell address to his neighbors at Springfield, Illinois, as he departs for Washington.

February 12; Abraham Lincoln's fifty-second birthday.

February 18; Inauguration of Jefferson Davis as President of the Confederate States of America.

February 22; Lincoln, at Philadelphia, warned of a plot to assassinate him while passing through Baltimore by Allan Pinkerton, chief of the Secret Service.

February 22; Lincoln speaks in Independence Hall at Philadelphia; abandons his public journey and makes a secret and hasty departure in the night from Harrisburg for Washington.

February 23; Lincoln arrives at Washington.

February 28; Congress organizes the territory of Colorado.

March 2; Congress organizes the territories of Nevada and Dakota.

March 4; Abraham Lincoln of Illinois is inaugurated the sixteenth President of the United States.

March 4; President Lincoln delivers his inaugural message and announces a change of administrative policy.

March 11; Confederate Congress provides for organization of an army.

April 12; Confederates open fire on Fort Sumter at 4.40 A. M.

April 14; Major Anderson evacuates Fort Sumter.

April 15; Lincoln calls for an extra session of Congress and 75,000 volunteer soldiers.

April 17; Virginia, the eighth state, secedes.

April 18; First volunteer troops reach Washington.

April 19; First bloodshed in the Civil War, on streets of Baltimore, Maryland.

April 29; Maryland house of delegates rejects ordinance of secession.

May 3; Lincoln calls for 500,000 volunteers; 700,680 respond.

May 6; Arkansas, the ninth state, seceded.

May 10; Lincoln proclaims martial law.

May 20; North Carolina, the tenth state, secedes.

June 3; Death of Stephen A. Douglas, age forty-eight, on the eve of the Civil War.

June 8; Tennessee, the eleventh state, secedes.

June 11; Forty counties in western part of Virginia repudiate secession ordinance and proclaim themselves a new state.

July 21; Confederates win battle of Bull Run.

July 22; Federal Congress votes $500,000,-000 to support the war, and gives Lincoln war-powers.

July 27; General George B. McClellan appointed to the command of the Army of the Potomac.

1861—November 8; Trent Affair—Mason and Slidell, Confederate Commissioners, taken from English ship, and England threatens war. Mason and Slidell are released.

1862—January 13; Lincoln calls Stanton to his cabinet as Secretary of War.

February 12; Abraham Lincoln's fifty-third birthday.

February 16; First great victory of the Federal arms; capture of Fort Donelson.

February 20; Abraham Lincoln's son, William Wallace Lincoln, age twelve, dies in the White House.

February 25; Congress passed Legal Tender Act.

March 9; Ironclad "Monitor" repulses the Confederate battleship "Merrimac" in four hours' naval combat.

April 4; Beginning of Peninsula Campaign.

April 6-7; Confederate attack on Pittsburg Landing repulsed.

April 16; Confederate Congress passed Conscription Acts, calling to military service all able-bodied persons between 18-45 years of age.

April 16; Slaves in District of Columbia emancipated by Congress.

April 25; Farragut wrests New Orleans from Confederates after desperate battle.

June 28; Conference of loyal governors at Altoona, Pennsylvania.

July 2; Lincoln calls for 300,000 volunteers for three years.

August 4; Lincoln calls for 300,000 militia for nine months.

August 30; Second defeat of the Federals at Second Bull Run.

August 31; General Fremont (Federal) ordered slaves freed in Missouri, but Lincoln modified proclamation.

September 17; Federal army victorious at battle of Antietam.

September 22; Lincoln issues the Emancipation Proclamation.

October 1; Lincoln visits the battlefield of Antietam.

October 4; Confederates defeated at Corinth.

December 13; Battle of Fredericksburg.

December 19; Attempt of the Senate to reconstruct the Cabinet.

December 31; Beginning of three days' battle at Murfreesboro.

1863—January 1; Emancipation Proclamation takes effect and slaves are declared free.

February 12; Abraham Lincoln's fifty-fourth birthday.

February 25; Congress established a national currency: National Bank Act passed by Congress.

March 3; Draft Act passed calling every able-bodied citizen of the United States into military service.

May 2-3; Federal army retreats at battle of Chancellorsville.

June 19; West Virginia, the thirty-fifth state, admitted to the Union.

July 1-3; Federal army wins battle of Gettysburg.

July 4; Federal army captures Vicksburg.

Chronology of the Life of Lincoln—1863-1865

1863—July 11; Washington threatened by Confederate hosts at its threshold.

July 13-16; Riots in New York City in opposition to Draft Act—about a thousand persons killed; a million and a half dollars' worth of property destroyed.

July 16; Second Conscription Act passed by Confederate Congress.

August 6; National Thanksgiving was observed for Union victories.

September 19-20; Federal army defeated at Chickamauga.

October 17; Lincoln calls for 300,000 volunteers.

November 19; Lincoln delivers his immortal eulogy at the battlefield of Gettysburg.

November 23-25; Federal army wins battle of Chattanooga.

1864—February 12; Abraham Lincoln's fifty-fifth birthday.

March 9; Grant made Commander-in-Chief of Federal forces.

May 5-12; Battles of the Wilderness.

June 14; The beginning of the siege of Petersburg, Virginia.

June 28; Secretary of the Treasury Chase resigns.

July 3; Delaware placed under martial law.

July 18; Lincoln calls for 500,000 men.

July 18; Conference at Niagara Falls of Horace Greeley and Confederate Commissioners.

September 2; Federals capture Atlanta.

October 31; Nevada, the thirty-sixth state, admitted to the Union.

November 8; Abraham Lincoln re-elected President of the United States; (Republican) 2,216,067; George B. McClellan (Democrat) 1,808,725.

December 10-21; Federal army captures Savannah.

December 15-16; Federal army wins battle of Nashville.

December 19; Lincoln calls for 300,000 volunteers.

1865—February 1; Thirteenth Amendment, constitutionally prohibiting slavery, adopted by Congress and ratified by states December 18, 1865.

February 3; Peace conference between Confederates and Federals at Hampton Roads, Virginia.

February 9; General Robert E. Lee made Commander-in-Chief of Confederate forces.

February 12; Abraham Lincoln's fifty-sixth birthday.

March 4; Lincoln delivers his second inaugural address.

1865—March 5; First negro ever entertained at White House—Frederick Douglas.

March 22 to April 9; Lincoln visits Grant's army at City Point, in Virginia.

April 3; Fall of Richmond, the capital of the Confederacy.

April 4-5; President Lincoln visits the ruins of the evacuated city of Richmond.

April 9; Surrender of Lee to Grant at Appomattox, Virginia.

April 11; Lincoln delivers his last speech from one of the windows at the White House.

April 14; Lincoln shot at Ford's Theater by John Wilkes Booth, the actor; the nation thrown into consternation.

April 14; Secretary of State, Seward, stabbed in bed. Failure of plot to assassinate General Grant and Vice-President Johnson.

April 15; Death of Abraham Lincoln at the hour of 7:22 on Saturday morning; the republic bows in grief; the world extends condolences.

April 15; Andrew Johnson of Tennessee takes oath of office as seventeenth President of the United States.

April 19; Funeral of Abraham Lincoln at the the White House; body borne to the National Capitol, to lie in state; memorial services held throughout the nation attended by more than 25,000,000 mourners.

April 21; Funeral train bearing remains of Lincoln leaves Washington; journey of nearly 2,000 miles; one of the greatest funeral pageants that the world had ever known.

April 26; John Wilkes Booth, assassinator of Lincoln, shot by " Boston " Corbett, cavalry sergeant, in Garrett's tobacco-house, near Bowling Green, in Virginia.

May 3; Arrival of funeral cortege of Lincoln at Springfield, Illinois, a million Americans having looked upon the face of the nation's savior.

May 4; Burial of Lincoln at " Oak Ridge " near his old home in Illinois; the press of the world paid tribute in eulogies to him as " the Greatest American."

May 12; Trial of conspirators in assassination plot begins. General Grant one of the first witnesses.

July 5; Mrs. Mary A. Surratt, Davey Herold, George A. Atzerodt and Lewis Payne found guilty and sentenced to be executed. Michael O'Laughlin, Sam Arnold and Dr. Samuel A. Mudd sentenced to life imprisonment. Edward Spangler sentenced to imprisonment for 6 years.

July 7; Hanging of Mrs. Surratt, Herold, Atzerodt and Payne in prison yard at Washington, as conspirators in the assassination of Lincoln.

Thy task is done; the bond are free:
   We bear thee to an honored grave,
Whose proudest monument shall be
   The broken fetters of the slave.

Pure was thy life; its bloody close
   Hath placed thee with the sons of light,
Among the noble host of those
   Who perished in the cause of Right.
            —William Cullen Bryant.

The Portrait Life of Lincoln

PART VI

A Handbook of the Famous Photographic
Portraits of Abraham Lincoln
Treasured in the Great American Collections

Famous Portraits of Abraham Lincoln

Page

First portrait taken of Lincoln when he entered National politics—age 37. This daguerreotype is undoubtedly first time that Lincoln sat for his portrait. It was taken during his campaign for Congress or shortly after his election, when he delivered his first speech—from 1846 to 1848. Photograph from original daguerreotype in possession of Honorable Robert T. Lincoln of Chicago, Illinois.. 13

Photograph of Mary Todd, who married Abraham Lincoln, in 1842—Lincoln was now 33 years of age. This negative was taken some years later, at time of Lincoln's inauguration for Presidency, and presents her in gown worn at Inaugural Ball—Original life negative in collection of Americana—Owned by Mr. Frederick H. Meserve of New York......... 15

Photograph taken while Lincoln, age 45, was engaged in Missouri Compromise, in 1854. Original was taken in an itinerant gallery in Chicago, for George Schneider, editor of "Staats Zeitung".. 17

Photograph taken in 1856 when Lincoln, age 47, was mentioned for Vice-President in first Republican Convention—Print in collection of Mr. Osborn H. Oldroyd of Washington, D. C.. 17

First photograph of Lincoln circulated throughout the country for campaign purposes—Taken in Chicago, in 1857—Lincoln was now 48 years of age. Original negative, by Alexander Hesler, burned in Chicago fire. Print in collection of Mr. H. W. Fay of DeKalb, Illinois.. 19

Ambrotype taken in 1858, shortly after Lincoln's speech at Galesburg, Illinois. Print owned by Mr. O. H. Oldroyd of Washington.. 19

Photograph Lincoln sat for in Springfield, Illinois, during the memorable campaign of 1858— age 49 years. Print owned by Mrs. Harriet Chapman of Charleston, Illinois........... 21

Ambrotype taken at Pittsfield, Illinois, October 1, 1858, immediately after Lincoln had made his speech on public square—age 49. Original by C. Jackson, owned by Miss Hattie Gilmer of Pittsfield, Illinois. Print in collection of Frederick H. Meserve, New York.. 21

Photograph of Stephen A. Douglas, taken during his debates with Lincoln in 1858—Lincoln was now 49 years of age; Douglas was 45 years. This negative was taken after Douglas defeated Lincoln for United States Senate, which was followed two years later by Lincoln's defeat of Douglas for President of the United States. Original in the collection of American celebrities—Owned by Mr. L. C. Handy of Washington, D. C......... 23

Ambrotype taken August 25, 1858, at Macomb, Illinois, when Lincoln was campaigning against Douglas for United States Senate—Owned by Mr. W. J. Franklin of Macomb, Illinois.... 25

Photograph of Lincoln as he appeared in political campaign, in 1858—age 49—Original negative owned by Dr. McWilliams of Dwight, Illinois. Print in possession of Mr. Stuart Brown of Springfield, Illinois.. 25

Ambrotype of Lincoln in linen coat, during Douglas debates at Beardstown, Illinois, in 1858— Original now in Lincoln Monument Collection at Springfield, Illinois—Print in possession of Mr. Osborn H. Oldroyd of Washington, D. C.. 27

Photograph taken during famous Lincoln-Douglas debates, in 1858—age 49—Collection of Mr. J. C. Browne of Philadelphia.. 27

Photograph of Lincoln at time of John Brown's raid, at Harper's Ferry—age 50—This negative, taken in 1859, was destroyed in Chicago fire—Mrs. Lincoln considered it best likeness of her husband she had ever seen—It presents Lincoln as he appeared just before his nomination for Presidency—Original negative by S. M. Fassett of Chicago, Illinois—Photograph owned by Mr. William Lloyd Garrison of Boston, Massachusetts—Print in collection of Mr. H. W. Fay of DeKalb, Illinois.. 29

Photograph of Lincoln taken in 1860 at the time of his "Cooper Institute Speech" in New York during his campaign for the Presidency—age 51—Original negative by Mathew Brady of New York—Collection of Mr. L. C. Handy of Washington, D. C.. 31

Photograph taken in summer of 1860 for campaign purposes—Original negative owned by Mr. M. C. Tuttle of St. Paul, Minnesota—Print from collection of Mr. Daniel Fish of Minneapolis, Minnesota.. 31

Photograph taken before the Republican National Convention at Chicago, in 1860—Found in collection of the late Mr. J. Henry Brown of Philadelphia.. 33

Photograph taken at his home in Springfield, Illinois, immediately after his nomination for Presidency, in 1860—age 51—Original by Alexander Hesler of Chicago, destroyed during the fire—Print in collection of Mr. Herbert W. Fay of DeKalb, Illinois................ 33

Photograph taken at Springfield, Illinois, in June, 1860—Copyright, 1894, by Mr. George B. Ayers—Negative now owned by Mr. H. C. Brown of New York........................ 35

Ambrotype taken at Springfield, Illinois, May 20, 1860—Original presented to Governor Marcus L. Ward of New Jersey—Now in possession of the Ward family of Newark, New Jersey. 35

Photograph of Lincoln as he entered campaign for Presidency at 51 years of age—Original negative taken in June, 1860, at Springfield, Illinois—Copyright, 1881, by Mr. George B. Ayers—Negative now owned by Mr. H. C. Brown of New York........................ 37

Ambrotype taken August, 1860, when seventy thousand Westerners visited Lincoln at his home in Springfield, Illinois—Age 51 years—Original in collection of Mr. William H. Lambert of Philadelphia.. 37

Famous Portraits of Abraham Lincoln

Page

Photograph of Lincoln greeting his neighbors for last time at his old home—Photograph taken at Springfield, Illinois, in 1861, when Lincoln was bidding farewell to his townspeople before going to inauguration at Washington—Negative in the collection of Americana, owned by Mr. F. H. Meserve of New York.................................... 39

Photograph of Capitol at Washington when Lincoln went to his inauguration—Photograph taken while crowd was gathering for inauguration, in 1861, showing National Capitol of Republic in course of its construction—Negative in collection of Americana, owned by Mr. Frederick H. Meserve of New York...................... 40

Photograph of Lincoln at his home in Springfield—Photograph taken early in 1861 as Lincoln stood with his two younger sons in his front yard—Print in collection of Mr. L. C. Handy of Washington... 41

Photograph of White House as Lincoln entered it—Photograph taken at Presidential mansion in Washington, in 1861, in first spring of Lincoln's occupancy—Print in collection of Mr. L. C. Handy of Washington................................... 41

Photograph taken shortly after Lincoln's election to the Presidency. Believed to be his first portrait with beard, early in 1861, at 52 years of age—Owned by Mr. H. W. Fay, DeKalb, Illinois... 43

Photograph taken at Springfield, Illinois, just prior to Lincoln's departure for Washington, in 1861—Original negative by F. M. McNulta—Now owned and copyrighted, 1894, by Mr. Herbert Wells Fay of DeKalb, Illinois........................ 43

Photograph of Lincoln taken early in 1861, about time he entered White House—Original negative by Alexander Hesler of Chicago—Print owned by Mr. Frank A. Brown of Minneapolis.. 45

Photograph of Lincoln taken just before leaving Springfield for White House, in 1861, age 52—Original negative by C. S. German—Print owned by Mr Allen Jasper Conant........ 45

Photograph of Lincoln at his inauguration—Negative taken while Lincoln was delivering inaugural address before great throng that had gathered at National Capitol—The judges of the Supreme Court can be seen sitting at his left—Print in the Brady-Gardner Collection deposited at Springfield, Massachusetts................................. 47

Photographs of members of President Lincoln's Cabinet—Original negatives taken from 1861-1865 by Mathew Brady of Washington 49-55

Photograph of Lincoln's Vice-President in 1861-1865—Hannibal Hamlin of Maine.......... 49

Photograph of Lincoln's Secretary of War in 1861-1862—Simon Cameron of Pennsylvania ... 49

Photograph of Lincoln's Secretary of War in 1862-1865—Edwin M. Stanton of Ohio 49

Photograph of Lincoln's Secretary of State in 1861-1865—William H. Seward of New York . 49

Photograph of Lincoln's Secretary of the Treasury in 1861-1864—Salmon P. Chase of Ohio ... 51

Photograph of Lincoln's Secretary of the Navy in 1861-1865—Gideon Welles of Connecticut .. 51

Photograph of Lincoln's Secretary of the Interior in 1861-1865—Caleb B. Smith of Indiana .. 51

Photograph of Lincoln's Postmaster-General in 1861-1864—Montgomery Blair of Maryland.. 51

Photograph of Lincoln's Attorney-General in 1861-1863—Edward Bates of Missouri 53

Photograph of Lincoln's Assistant Secretary of War—Charles A. Dana of New York....... 53

Photograph of Lincoln's Secretary of the Treasury in 1864-1865—William P. Fessenden of Maine 53

Photograph of Lincoln's Secretary of the Interior in 1863-1865—John P. Usher of Indiana 53

Photograph of Lincoln's Secretary of the Treasury in 1865—Hugh McCulloch of Indiana.... 55

Photograph of Lincoln's Attorney-General in 1864-1865—James Speed of Kentucky 55

Photograph of Lincoln's Postmaster-General in 1864-1865—William Dennison of Ohio 55

Photograph of Lincoln's Second Vice-President in 1865—Andrew Johnson of North Carolina. 55

Photograph of Lincoln seated with his Secretaries, Nicolay and Hay—Taken in Springfield, Illinois, in 1861, just before leaving for Washington—Print in original Brady-Gardner Collection at Springfield, Massachusetts.................................... 57

Photograph presented by Lincoln to Mrs. Lucy G. Speed, on October 3, 1861, on which he inscribed his autograph—Negative in the collection of Americana in possession of Mr. Frederick H. Meserve of New York...................................... 57

Photograph of Lincoln in camp with army at Antietam—Negative taken October 3, 1862, when Lincoln was standing in front of General McClellan's tent—Taken by Mathew Brady, government photographer—Original negative in the Brady Collection at Springfield, Massachusetts—Copyrighted, 1910, by the Patriot Publishing Company................ 59

Photograph of President Lincoln on battlefield of Antietam under guard of the Secret Service—Original negative taken by Mathew Brady on October 3, 1862; Lincoln was accompanied by Allan Pinkerton (Major Allen), first chief of the Secret Service, standing at his right, and General McClernand at his left—Deposited in the Original Collection of seven thousand negatives valued at $150,000 at Springfield, Massachusetts—Copyright, 1907, by Mr. Edward Bailey Eaton, Hartford, Connecticut.............................. 60

Famous Portraits of Abraham Lincoln

Page

Photograph of Lincoln with his Generals—Original negative taken in Army of the Potomac at Antietam, on October 3, 1862, while Lincoln was addressing General McClellan and staff—Negative in Brady-Gardner Collection at Springfield, Massachusetts—Copyright, 1907, by Mr. Edward Bailey Eaton, Hartford, Connecticut................. 61

Photograph of Lincoln with his soldiers at battle-line—Negative taken while Lincoln was inspecting conditions in army at Antietam on October 3, 1862—Original negative by Mathew Brady—Print in collection of Mr. C. M. Derickson of Monessen, Pennsylvania 61

Photograph of President Lincoln in General McClellan's tent at battle grounds of Antietam— Original negative taken by Mathew Brady on October 3, 1862, while Lincoln was in conference with General McClellan a few days after the great battle—Now deposited in the Brady-Gardner Collection at Springfield, Massachusetts—Copyright, 1907, by Mr. Edward Bailey Eaton and valued at ten thousand dollars.................... 62

Photograph of President Lincoln in the second year of the American Civil War—Original negative taken by Mathew Brady in Washington, in 1862—Print owned by Mr. Baldwin Coolidge of Boston, Massachusetts..................... 63

Photograph taken after first Emancipation Proclamation—Original negative by Mathew Brady at Washington in September, 1862, age 53 years—Print in possession of Mr. L. C. Handy of Washington, District of Columbia.................... 65

Photograph of Lincoln shortly after signing of Emancipation Proclamation—Original negative taken by Alexander Gardner at Washington, in 1863, when Lincoln, age 54, broke the chains that had bound three million slaves—Negative in collection of Americana of Frederick H. Meserve, New York..................... 67

Photograph of President Lincoln's son, William Wallace Lincoln, who died in White House, February 20, 1862, at twelve years of age—Collection of Mr. Frederick H. Meserve of New York..................... 69

Photograph of Thomas (Tad) Lincoln, born April 4, 1853, who became companion of President Lincoln during his last years in White House—The oldest son, Robert Todd Lincoln, was in Harvard—Collection of Frederick H. Meserve.................... 69

Photograph of Lincoln taken at Washington, in 1863, shortly after battle of Chancellorsville— Original negative by Mathew Brady..................... 71

Photograph taken the Sunday before Lincoln left for battlefield of Gettysburg in November, 1863—Original negative by Mathew Brady..................... 71

Photograph taken during Lincoln's speech on battlefield of Gettysburg—Original negative by Alexander Gardner on November 19, 1863, while Lincoln was delivering his famous Gettysburg address at consecration of the cemetery—Original in Brady-Gardner Collection at Springfield, Massachusetts—Copyrighted, 1910, by the Patriot Publishing Company..................... 73

Photograph taken about time of battle of Gettysburg, in 1863—Original negative by Mathew Brady..................... 74

Photograph taken in Brady Gallery at National Capital, in 1863, during darkest days of Civil War—Original negative by Mathew Brady—Life negative in collection of Americana of Frederick H. Meserve of New York..................... 74

Photograph taken shortly after Lincoln called for a half million more men, in 1864—Original negative by Mathew Brady of Washington..................... 75

Photograph taken when Lincoln was seeking a new general for all the armies of the Republic, in 1864—Negative by Mathew Brady at Washington..................... 75

Photograph of Lincoln taken early in 1864 at request of Secretary Seward of his cabinet— Original negative by Mathew Brady at Washington—Now in the collection of Mr. L. C. Handy at Washington..................... 77

Photograph taken about time of battle of Spottsylvania Court House, in 1864—Original negative by Mathew Brady—Deposited in the War Department Collection at Washington.. 77

Photograph of Lincoln about time Lincoln met Grant, in 1864—Original negative by Mathew Brady at Washington—Life negative in collection of Mr. Frederick H. Meserve of New York..................... 79

Photograph of Lincoln about time of Grant's taking command of the army, in 1864—Original negative by Mathew Brady—Print in collection of Mr. Frederick H. Meserve of New York 79

Photograph of Lincoln about time of his second nomination for Presidency of United States— Negative taken in 1864, when political leaders were declaring that Lincoln could not be re-elected and American people were demanding his leadership—Original negative by Walker of Washington—Print from the collection of Mr. Osborn H. Oldroyd at the Lincoln Museum at Washington..................... 81

Photograph of Lincoln at time of his second nomination for Presidency, in 1864—Original negative by Mathew Brady—From collection of Americana of Frederick H. Meserve of New York..................... 82

Photograph of Lincoln with his son Thomas (Tad), in 1864—Original negative by Mathew Brady at Washington..................... 82

Famous Portraits of Abraham Lincoln

Page

Photograph of Lincoln with his son Thomas (Tad) in White House—Negative taken with Lincoln in his characteristic attitude at home with his eleven-year-old son by his side—His son William Wallace had died at the White House two years before—Original negative by Mathew Brady in collection of Mr. L. C. Handy at Washington 83

Photograph of Lincoln about time of second election as President, in 1864—Original negative by Walker, photographer for the Treasury Department at Washington—Print from collection of Mr. Frederick H. Meserve of New York......................... 85

Photograph of Lincoln, age 56 years, shortly before his second inauguration, in 1865—Original negative by Alexander Gardner at Washington—Print from the collection of Mr. Frederick H. Meserve of New York......................... 85

Photograph of Lincoln in closing days of American Crisis, in 1865—Original negative by Alexander Gardner at Washington—Print from the collection of Mr. L. C. Handy in Washington, District of Columbia........................ 87

Photograph of Lincoln at his second inauguration, in 1865, age 56 years—Original negative by H. F. Warren, Waltham, Massachusetts—Print in the collection of Mr. Osborn H. Oldroyd at the Lincoln Museum in Washington........................ 87

Photograph of President Lincoln about time of fall of Richmond, in 1865—Original negative taken a few days before Lincoln went to capital of Confederacy to look upon ruins of historic city—Original negative by Mathew Brady—Deposited in Original Brady Collection at Springfield, Massachusetts—Copyright, 1909, by Mr. Edward Bailey Eaton.... 89

Photograph of Lincoln at end of Civil War and Surrender at Appomattox—Original negative taken in Washington, in 1865, shortly before the hosts of the South and the legions of the North clasped hands in peace—Original negative by Mathew Brady, now considered the greatest portrait of Lincoln ever taken—Deposited in the Original Brady Collection at Springfield, Massachusetts—Copyright, 1908, by Mr. Edward Bailey Eaton 91

Last portrait of Lincoln ever taken—Photograph taken a few days before end of Lincoln's life, in April, 1865, when war was over and American people were re-united into an inseparable brotherhood—Original negative by Alexander Gardner at Washington—Collection of Mr. M. P. Rice of Washington—Copyright, 1891........................ 93

Photograph taken at Ford's Theater in Washington, after assassination on night of April 14, 1865—Original negative by Alexander Gardner—Now deposited in the Original Brady Collection of seven thousand negatives, at Springfield, Massachusetts 97

Photograph of President Lincoln's box in Ford's Theater as it appeared on night of tragedy 97

Photograph of chair in which President Lincoln was sitting when shot by John Wilkes Booth 97

Photograph of house in which President Lincoln died on Saturday morning, April 15, 1865—Photograph taken of building opposite Ford's Theater in which Lincoln spent last hours—The house is now the famous Lincoln Museum established by Mr. Osborn H. Oldroyd at Washington, D. C.—Print in possession of Mr. L. C. Handy of Washington................. 99

Photograph of John Wilkes Booth, actor, who shot Lincoln at Ford's Theater, Friday night, April 14, 1865........................ 101

Photograph of Sergeant Boston Corbett, 16th New York Cavalry, who fired shot that killed fugitive Booth in a barn in Virginia, at 3.15 a. m., April 26, 1865—Negatives in Original Brady-Gardner Collection at Springfield, Massachusetts....................... 101

Photographs of conspirators hanged for assassination of Lincoln—Original Secret Service negatives in Brady-Gardner Collection at Springfield, Massachusetts...................... 102

Photograph of Mrs. Mary E. Surratt, an unfortunate widow and mother, whose home unwittingly became the center of the conspiracy 102

Photograph of George Atzerodt, carriage painter, who, it was charged, was delegated to assassinate Vice-President Johnson....................... 102

Photograph of Davey Herold, boy who aided Booth to escape, and left his mother and seven sisters heartbroken........................ 102

Photograph of Lewis Payne (Powell), a Florida boy, in double irons. He attempted to assassinate Seward at his home........................ 102

Photographs of accessories imprisoned for assassination of Lincoln—Original Secret Service negatives in the Brady-Gardner Collection at Springfield, Massachusetts................ 103

Photograph of Michael O'Laughlin, sentenced for life and died during imprisonment; his remains were sent to his mother....................... 103

Photograph of Samuel Arnold, clerk in sutler's store, sentenced for life and pardoned after serving four years....................... 103

Photograph of Edward Spangler, scene shifter, sentenced to six years; pardoned in four years, and died eighteen months later....................... 103

Photograph of Dr. Samuel A. Mudd, physician, who, for harboring Booth, was sentenced for life; pardoned after four years........................ 103

Famous Portraits of Abraham Lincoln

Page

Photograph of prison where conspirators were confined—Negative taken at old penitentiary building on arsenal grounds at Washington, where accused were imprisoned in cells and heavily chained and manacled—Original negative in Brady-Gardner Collection deposited in Springfield, Massachusetts.. 104

Photograph of Military Court that tried Lincoln conspirators—Negative taken when commission began to take testimony on May 12, 1865—Lieutenant-General Grant, whose life was also in conspiracy, was first witness—Print in collection of Americana of Mr. Frederick H. Meserve of New York...... 104

Photograph of gallows in prison yard where conspirators were hanged—Negative taken on afternoon of July 7, 1865, when ropes were being noosed about conspirators—Original negative by Alexander Gardner, government photographer, now in Brady-Gardner Collection in Springfield, Massachusetts.. 105

Photograph of execution of convicted prisoners in Lincoln assassination—This remarkable negative is silent witness of end of one of the world's greatest tragedies—Taken by Alexander Gardner while those who paid penalty were hanging on gallows—Negative in Springfield, Massachusetts.. 105

Photograph of funeral procession of Lincoln passing through streets of Washington at beginning of sixteen hundred mile journey to his old home at Springfield, Illinois, on April 21, 1865—Negative by Gardner..................................... 107

Photograph of bier on which President Lincoln rested in state while men, women, and children wept over their lost leader on his funeral day on April 19, 1865, when twenty-five million people throughout country bowed their heads in tribute—Original negatives by Alexander Gardner now deposited in Brady-Gardner Collection at Springfield, Massachusetts...... 107

Photograph of funeral catafalque of Lincoln passing through Philadelphia.................. 108

Photograph while Lincoln's body was lying in state before great throngs at City Hall in New York.. 108

Photograph of the funeral car bearing the dead Lincoln back to Springfield, Illinois—Prints from the collection of Mr. Frederick H. Meserve of New York...................... 108

Photograph taken while laying Lincoln in his tomb in beautiful Oak Ridge Cemetery in Springfield, Illinois, on May 4, 1865.. 109

Photograph of tomb of Lincoln where Lincoln's body was left with a soldier's guard by a mourning nation—Prints from the collection of Mr. Frederick H. Meserve of New York.. 109

Photograph of national memorial at Lincoln's burial place in his old home city of Springfield, Illinois—Massive marble column rising above the catacomb and memorial hall proclaims the simple greatness of the man whom the whole world loves—Photograph taken shortly after its erection, in 1874, showing the original tomb at the foot of the hill where Lincoln lay for nine years—Print in collection of Americana owned by Mr. Frederick H. Meserve of New York.. 110

This collection includes all the original photographs of Abraham Lincoln that are known to be in existence. In many instances the original negatives have been destroyed and prints are in possession of several collectors. It has been the desire of this handbook to give the credit to the owner of the original negative whenever it is known to be in existence. Otherwise the credit is given to the collection from which the print used in this volume is taken. During the exhaustive investigations necessary in making this collection it was found that various coyprights on the same print are held by several collectors, while the holder of the original negative seems to be unprotected. While there has been considerable democracy in copyright protections, it is not probable that the collector holding merely a print has an equitable right to control another man's property. This condition is probably partially due to the kinship which Abraham Lincoln holds to the American people—a kinship which has made his portraits a common heritage of the generations. The actual property right is undoubtedly with the owner of the original negative. It has been the desire of the investigator, however, to fully respect the claims of the various collectors and to give them full credit for the courtesy that they have extended without entering into their conflicting claims.

Hundred Greatest Books on Abraham Lincoln

Abraham Lincoln, A History—By his secretaries, John C. Nicolay and John Hay—A monumental work in ten volumes, portraying the life of a man and the history of the times from intimate association.

History and Personal Recollections of Abraham Lincoln—By his law partner, William H. Herndon, assisted by Jesse William Weik—A true story of a great life by one who was with him when he rose from obscurity—Recorded in two volumes.

Life of Abraham Lincoln—By Ida Minerva Tarbell—Testimony of many witnesses who knew Lincoln in his early life, with reminiscences by his friends, including many exhibits of rare documents, speeches, letters and telegrams—Recorded in two volumes.

The Everyday Life of Abraham Lincoln—By Francis F. Browne—Lincoln's life and character portrayed by those who knew him; the friends, neighbors and associates during his whole career—Estimates and impressions of distinguished men, with reminiscences, incidents, and tributes from universal sources.

The True Abraham Lincoln—By William Eleroy Curtis—Entertaining and graphic pictures of Lincoln from men who knew him—The simple story of a common man.

Abraham Lincoln, The Man of the People—By Norman Hapgood—Story of a man who became the leader of the plain people—A virile expression of the character of Lincoln and qualities that made him the greatest man of his times and yet the simplest and most humble.

Abraham Lincoln, The Boy and the Man—By James Morgan—A dramatic story of the struggles and troubles of the common man; how he solved great problems by the plain reasoning of common sense and wrought great deeds by the exercise of the common qualities of honesty and courage, patience, justice and conscience.

Abraham Lincoln, American Statesman—By John Torrey Morse—An able and critical study of Lincoln and his work—An estimate of his statesmanship and political greatness, in two volumes.

The Life of Abraham Lincoln—By Isaac Newton Arnold—An entertaining narrative by the lawyer who was associated with Lincoln at the bar of Illinois and as a member of Congress in war time—The same author wrote *The History of Abraham Lincoln and the Overthrow of Slavery*, immediately after Lincoln's death, in 1866.

The Life of Abraham Lincoln from His Birth to His Inauguration as President—By Ward Hill Lamon—Personal recollections of Lincoln's law partner at Springfield, who, after Lincoln's election as President, became his private secretary and later his marshal—His recollections have also been edited by his daughter, Dorothy Lamon.

The Life and Public Services of Abraham Lincoln, Sixteenth President of the United States—By Henry Jarvis Raymond, who himself took a prominent part in the politics of the times—This is one of the first biographies of Lincoln and appeared in 1864-5, given with state papers, speeches, messages, letters, and intimate descriptions of the closing scenes connected with his life and death.

The Life of Abraham Lincoln—By Joseph Gilbert Holland, one of the journalists who knew Lincoln intimately and was one of the first to write his biography in 1865-6—He was a Northerner who had lived in the South and knew the estimate of the man—His simple story is still one of just and honest judgment.

Six Months at the White House with Abraham Lincoln—By Francis B. Carpenter, an artist who painted one of the famous portraits of Lincoln and lived with him during the most critical days of the American Crisis, portraying the inner life at the White House—This is an intimate story written in 1866.

Life on the Circuit with Lincoln—By Henry Clay Whitney, a fellow circuit rider who knew the simple manhood of Lincoln as the country lawyer—A characterized portrayal of Lincoln in his most picturesque background.

Recollections of Abraham Lincoln—By Lucius Eugene Chittenden, an official in Lincoln's administration who gives his personal reminiscences and experiences with the President during the war—Entertaining memories of one who was close to Lincoln in Washington.

Lincoln, Master of Men—By Alonzo Rothschild—A study of the character of Lincoln and his ability as a leader—A brilliant estimate of his power, original in its treatment and executed with skill.

Personal Recollections of Abraham Lincoln and the Civil War—By James Roberts Gilmore—Entertaining glimpses into the personal characteristics of Lincoln with memoirs and anecdotes of personal relations with him during the dark days of the Civil War.

Washington in Lincoln's Time—By Noah Brooks, a trusted friend of Lincoln who was associated with the man and the events during the American Crisis—His books also include a biography of Lincoln for young people; a narrative of the worth and early manhood of Lincoln; and his connection with the downfall of slavery.

Abraham Lincoln, An Essay—By Carl Schurz, who was appointed minister to Spain by President Lincoln and later became a member of President Hayes' cabinet—A luminous appreciation, given with testimonies by Emerson, Whittier, Holmes and Lowell.

Complete Works of Abraham Lincoln—Twelve volumes containing several authentic lines known to be in existence from the speeches and writings of Lincoln, including his letters, state papers, and messages—With exhaustive Lincoln biography by Daniel Fish.

Hundred Greatest Books on Abraham Lincoln

Abraham Lincoln's Pen and Voice—Compiled by G. M. Van Buren—A complete compilation of his letters, civil, political, and military; also his public addresses, messages to Congress, inaugurals and others.

Abraham Lincoln's Speeches Complete—Edited by J. B. McClure—From his first address in Pappsville, Illinois, 1832, to his last address in Washington, April 11, 1865.

Abraham Lincoln, Stories and Speeches—Edited by J. B. McClure.

Lincoln's Early Speeches—Edited by Bliss Perry—Springfield speech—Cooper Union speech—Inaugural addresses—Gettysburg address—Selected letters—Lincoln's last speech.

Lincoln; Passages from His Speeches and Letters—With an introduction by R. W. Gilder.

The Table Talk of Abraham Lincoln—Edited by W. O. Stoddard.

Words of Abraham Lincoln—Selected, arranged and annotated by I. Thomas—For use in schools.

Words of Lincoln—Compiled by O. H. Oldroyd—With an introduction by M. W. Fuller and T. S. Hamlin—Including several hundred opinions of his life and character by eminent persons of this and other lands.

Political Debates Between Abraham Lincoln and Stephen A. Douglas—In the celebrated campaign of 1858 in Illinois; including the preceding speeches of each at Chicago, and Springfield.

Political Speeches and Debates of Abraham Lincoln and Stephen A. Douglas, 1854-1861—Edited by Alonzo T. Jones.

Abraham Lincoln, The Backwoods Boy—By Horatio Alger, Jr.—Story of how a Young Railsplitter became President—Boyhood and Manhood Series of Illustrious Americans.

Life of Abraham Lincoln—By Joseph H. Barrett—With a condensed view of his most important speeches, his messages, proclamations, letters, and a concise history of the war.

The Life and Public Services of Honorable Abraham Lincoln—By Davis Vandewater Golden Bartlett.

The True Story of Abraham Lincoln, the American, Told for Boys and Girls—Children's Lives of Great Men—By Elbridge Streeter Brooks.

In the Boyhood of Lincoln—By Hezekiah Butterworth.

Abraham Lincoln—By Charles Carleton Coffin.

Life of Abraham Lincoln, Sixteenth President of the United States—By Frank Crosby—Containing his early history and political career; together with his speeches, messages, proclamations and other official documents.

Greeley on Lincoln—Edited by Joel Benton—With Mr. Greeley's letter to Charles A. Dana and a lady friend—Added reminiscences of Horace Greeley.

Abraham Lincoln: His Life and Public Services—Narrative by a woman in 1865—By Phebe Ann Coffin Hanaford.

Assassination of Lincoln—By Thomas Mealey Harris—A history of the great conspiracy—Trial of the conspirators by a military commission and a review of the trial of John H. Surratt.

Nancy Hanks—By Caroline Hanks Hitchcock—The story of Abraham Lincoln's mother, Nancy Hanks.

Abraham Lincoln and the Abolition of Slavery in the United States—By Charles Godfrey Leland.

Abraham Lincoln and Men of War-Times—By Alexander Kelly McClure—Some personal recollections of war and politics during the Lincoln administration.

Anecdotes of Abraham Lincoln and Lincoln's Stories—By James B. McClure.

Life of Abraham Lincoln—By Clifton M. Nichols—Being a biography of Lincoln's life from his birth to his assassination; also a record of his ancestors, and a collection of anecdotes attributed to Lincoln.

The Assassination of Abraham Lincoln—By Osborn Hamiline Oldroyd—Flight, pursuit, capture, and punishment of the conspirators, with an introduction by T. M. Harris.

The Lincoln Memorial; Album-Immortelles—Collected and edited by O. H. Oldroyd—Original life-pictures, with autographs, from the hands and hearts of eminent Americans and Europeans, contemporaries of the great martyr to liberty, Abraham Lincoln; together with extracts from his speeches and sayings—With an introduction by M. Simpson, D. D., and a sketch of the patriot's life by I. N. Arnold.

Abraham Lincoln—By John Carroll Power—His life, public services, death and great funeral cortege, from Washington to Springfield, Illinois—With history and description of the national Lincoln monument—History of the attempt to steal the body of Abraham Lincoln—Including a history of the Lincoln guard of honor, with eight years Lincoln memorial services.

Lincoln in Story—By Silas Gamaliel Pratt—The life of the Martyr-President told in authenticated anecdotes.

The Children's Life of Abraham Lincoln—By M. Louise Putnam.

Reminiscences of Abraham Lincoln, By Distinguished Men of His Times—By Allen Thorndike Rice—Contains articles by Ulysses S. Grant, Elihu B. Washburne, George W. Julian, R. E. Fenton, J. P. Usher, George S. Boutwell, Benjamin F. Butler, Charles C. Coffin, Frederick Douglass, Lawrence Weldon, Benjamin P. Poore, Titian J. Coffey, Henry Ward Beecher, William D. Kelley, Cassius M. Clay, Robert G. Ingersoll, A. H. Markland, Schuyler Colfax,

Daniel W. Voorhees, Charles A. Dana, John A. Kasson, James B. Fry, Hugh McCulloch, Chauncey M. Depew, David R. Locke, Leonard Swett, Walt Whitman, Donn Piatt, E. W. Andrews, James C. Welling, John Conness, John B. Alley, and Thomas Hicks.

The First Published Life of Abraham Lincoln—By John Locke Scripps—Written in the year 1860; reprinted in the year 1900, by the Cranbrook Press.

The Life, Stories, and Speeches of Abraham Lincoln—By Paul Selby—A compilation of Lincoln's most remarkable utterances, with a sketch of his life.

Abraham Lincoln, A Character Sketch—By Robert Dickinson Sheppard—With anecdotes, characteristics and chronology.

Abraham Lincoln: The True Story of a Great Life—By William Osborn Stoddard—Showing the inner growth, special training and peculiar fitness of the man for his work—Also *Inside the White House in War-Times*, and *Lincoln at Work; Sketches from Life*.

Pioneer Home to the White House—By William Makepeace Thayer—Life of Abraham Lincoln—With Eulogy by Honorable George Bancroft—The Pioneer boy, and how he became President.

Abraham Lincoln, The First American—By David D. Thompson.

Tributes to the Memory of Abraham Lincoln—Reproduction in facsimile of eighty-seven memorials addressed by foreign municipalities and societies to the government of the United States—Prepared under the direction of the Secretary of State at Washington.

The Assassination of Abraham Lincoln; late President of the United States of America, and the attempted assassination of William H. Seward, Secretary of State, and Frederick W. Seward, Assistant Secretary, on the evening of the 14th of April, 1865—Expression of condolence and sympathy inspired by these events—Washington; Government Printing Office, 1867.

Abraham Lincoln, Tributes from His Associates—Reminiscences of soldiers, statesmen and citizens—By William Hayes Ward.

Complete Works of Abraham Lincoln—Edited by John G. Nicolay and John Hay; with a general introduction by Richard Watson Gilder, and special articles by other eminent persons.

Writings of Abraham Lincoln—Edited by Arthur Brooks Lapsley, with an introduction by Theodore Roosevelt; together with The Essay on Lincoln, by Carl Schurz; The Address on Lincoln, by Joseph H. Choate, and The Life of Lincoln, by Noah Brooks.

The Lincoln and Douglas Debates—The senatorial campaign of 1858 in Illinois, between Abraham Lincoln and Stephen Arnold Douglas; containing also Lincoln's address at Cooper Institute, with introduction and notes by Archibald Lewis Bouton.

Abraham Lincoln, a True Life—By James Baldwin.

The Lincoln Legion, the Story of Its Founder and Forerunners—By Louis Albert Banks.

Abraham Lincoln and His Presidency—By Joseph Hartwell Barrett.

The Genesis of Lincoln—By James H. Cathey—Truth is stranger than fiction.

Abraham Lincoln, The Liberator: A Biographical Sketch—By Charles Wallace French.

The Story of Abraham Lincoln—By Mrs. Eleanor Gridley—The journey from the log cabin to the White House.

"Abe" Lincoln's Yarns and Stories—By Alexander Kelly McClure—A complete collection of the funny and witty anecdotes that made Lincoln famous as America's greatest story teller; with introduction and anecdotes—The story of Lincoln's life told by himself in his stories.

The Real Lincoln—By Charles Landon Carter Minor—From the testimony of Lincoln's contemporaries.

Abraham Lincoln—By Ellis Paxson Oberholtzer—American Crisis Biographies.

Abraham Lincoln, A Character Sketch—By Robert Dickinson Sheppard—With Supplementary Essay—By G. Mercer Adam—Also *Suggestions from the Life of Lincoln*—By Prof. Francis W. Shepardson—*The Early Years of Abraham Lincoln*—By Prof. Goldwin Smith . . . together with anecdotes, characteristics, and chronology.

The Boy Lincoln—By William Osborn Stoddard.

Abraham Lincoln, the Pioneer Boy, and How He Became President—The story of his life—By William Makepeace Thayer.

A List of Lincolniana in the Library of Congress—By G. T. Ritchie—Writings of Abraham Lincoln—Writings relating to Abraham Lincoln—Washington; Government Printing Office, 1903.

Lincoln and the Freedmen—By J. Grant Eaton, in collaboration with Ethel Osgood Mason—Reminiscences of the Civil War, with special reference to the work for the contrabands and freedmen of the Mississippi Valley.

History of the Administration of President Lincoln—By H. J. Raymond—Including Lincoln's speeches, letters, proclamations and messages—With preliminary sketch of his life.

The Life of Dr. Samuel A. Mudd—By N. Mudd—Containing Dr. Mudd's letters from Fort Jefferson, Dry Tortugas Island, where he was imprisoned four years for alleged complicity in the assassination of Abraham Lincoln, with statements of Mrs. Samuel A. Mudd, Dr. Samuel A. Mudd, and Edward Spangler regarding the assassination and the argument of General Ewing on the question of the jurisdiction of the military commission, and on the law and facts of the case; also the "diary" of John Wilkes Booth.

Lincoln in the Telegraph Office—By D. H. Bates—Recollections of the United State military telegraph corps during the Civil War.

Lincoln the Lawyer—By F. T. Hill.

The Story-Life of Lincoln—By Wayne Whipple—A biography composed of five hundred true stories told by Abraham Lincoln and his friends, selected from all authentic sources.

The Memory of Lincoln—Poems selected, with an introduction by M. A. DeW. Howe, Boston, 1899.

The Lincoln Album; life of the preserver of the Union, the liberator of a people, and the first American—Told by authentic picture—Facsimile, letters, speeches, quotations, genealogy, and a chronological table giving the principal events of his career, with the dates of their occurrence.

The Lincoln Centennial Medal, presenting the medal of Abraham Lincoln by Jules Edouard Roine, together with papers on the medal.

Abraham Lincoln—By George Haven Putnam, Litt. D.—The People's leader in the struggle for national existence.

The Death of Lincoln—By Clara E. Laughlin—The story of Booth's plot, his deed and the penalty.

The Assassination of Abraham Lincoln and Its Expiation—By David Miller Dewitt.

O Captain! My Captain!

O Captain! my Captain! our fearful trip is done,
The ship has weather'd every rack, the prize we sought is won,
The port is near, the bells I hear, the people all exulting,
While follow eyes the steady keel, the vessel grim and daring;
    But O heart! heart! heart!
    O the bleeding drops of red,
      Where on the deck my Captain lies,
      Fallen cold and dead.

O Captain! my Captain! rise up and hear the bells;
Rise up—for you the flag is flung—for you the bugle trills,
For you bouquets and ribbon'd wreaths—for you the shores a-crowding,
For you they call, the swaying mass, their eager faces turning;
    Here Captain! dear father!
    This arm beneath your head!
      It is some dream that on the deck,
      You've fallen cold and dead.

My Captain does not answer, his lips are pale and still,
My father does not feel my arm, he has no pulse nor will,
The ship is anchor'd safe and sound, its voyage closed and done,
From fearful trip the victor ship comes in with object won;
    Exult O shores, and ring O bells!
    But I with mournful tread,
      Walk the deck my Captain lies,
      Fallen cold and dead.
               —*Walt Whitman.*